Arbeitsblätter

Vertretungsstunden Englisch in der Sekundarstufe I

60 Arbeitsblätter
mit Lösungsangaben

von
Regina Großkopf

Ernst Klett Verlag
Stuttgart Düsseldorf Leipzig

Gedruckt auf Papier, das aus Altpapier
hergestellt wurde.

Die Deutsche Bibliothek – CIP-Einheitsaufnahme
Großkopf, Regina:
Arbeitsblätter Vertretungsstunden Englisch in der Sekundarstufe I :
60 Arbeitsblätter mit Lösungsangaben / von Regina Großkopf. –
2. Aufl. – Stuttgart ; Düsseldorf ; Leipzig : Klett, 1999
ISBN 3-12-927895-8

2. Auflage 1999 A

Internetadresse: http://www.klett-verlag.de
E-Mail: klett-kundenservice@klett-mail.de
Umschlaggestaltung: BSS Werbeagentur Sachse und Partner, Bietigheim
Zeichnungen (außer A 23 und A 25): Sven Palmowski, Stuttgart.
Druck und Bindung: Wilhelm Röck, Weinsberg. Printed in Germany.
ISBN 3-12-927895-8

Zu diesem Band

Kurzfristig für eine erkrankte Lehrkraft in einer unbekannten Klasse einzuspringen, erfüllt manche Kollegen mit Unbehagen. Wie weit ist die entsprechende Klasse im Stoff fortgeschritten? Welche nächsten Schritte wären im Unterricht sinnvoll? Und Rücksprache mit der zu vertretenden Lehrkraft ist nicht möglich. Was tun?

Man begibt sich also auf die Suche nach geeignetem Material und ist vielfach enttäuscht. An Vorschlägen für Vertretungsstunden mangelt es zwar nicht, doch muss oft erst Vorarbeit geleistet werden – in der mitunter sehr kurzen Frist vor einer Vertretungsstunde eine nervenaufreibende Tätigkeit. Zudem scheint in Veröffentlichungen besonders zum Vetretungsunterricht in modernen Fremdsprachen eine Vorliebe für die Behandlung von Grammatikproblemen zu bestehen. Grammatikunterricht ist aber gerade in Vertretungsstunden bei Schülern besonders unbeliebt.

In Veröffentlichungen für andere Fächer wie Mathematik oder Deutsch findet sich dagegen eine bunte Vielfalt an Vorschlägen – Konzentrationsaufgaben, Puzzles, Denksportaufgaben usw.
Ich habe deshalb versucht, nun auch für das Fach Englisch eine möglichst abwechslungsreiche Sammlung von Kopiervorlagen zusammenzustellen, die bis auf wenige Ausnahmen sofort im Unterricht einsetzbar sind, eine sinnvolle Beschäftigung der Schüler und Schülerinnen ermöglichen und die darüber hinaus auch noch Spaß machen.

Die Lösungen finden sich im Anhang – sofern nötig durch kurze Kommentare ergänzt.

Die Arbeitsblätter nehmen unterschiedlich Zeit in Anspruch. Manche Schüler sind sehr findig beim Lösen solcher Aufgaben, andere brauchen mehr Zeit.
Die Blätter lassen sich auch im normalen Unterricht einsetzen: als Motivationsschub, zum Wiederholen von Wortschatz, zur Förderung der Kommunikation oder zur Schulung der Konzentration.

Da nicht in allen Schulen der einzelnen Bundesländer der Englischunterricht mit der fünften Klasse einsetzt, wurden die Arbeitsblätter nach Lernjahren und nicht nach Schuljahren aufgeteilt.
Diese Einteilung muss keinesfalls zwingend sein. So ist durchaus denkbar, dass Blätter für das 5./6. Lernjahr auch schon im 4. Lernjahr von den Schülern gern durchgearbeitet werden. Und einige Vorschläge für frühere Lernjahre dürften auch noch bei weiter fortgeschrittenen Schülerinnen und Schülern gut ankommen.

Regina Großkopf

Cross out some letters and find words. (They must have four letters or more. But do not change the order of the letters!) The longest words are the best.

1. BI~~L~~~~C~~R~~E~~O   biro
2. BLINSATENRS ______
3. ERWITOMPLAN ______
4. ALFOTERINOSON ______
5. STWAINTRDLOW ______
6. BROSEHCIRND ______
7. BALROSTCHIER ______
8. REFPNOGLISCH ______
9. TRERSRISBOLE ______
10. OFRAMBILYER ______
11. UNPBSOTAGIRTS ______
12. SUTCNODIERS ______
13. WASRTORNPAG ______
14. STAEARCTHIER ______
15. SOWRTALINKS ______
16. GRETROMFLANT ______
17. TEALSEPTHORNDE ______
18. TAHESIRWETALR ______
19. WAHESRENELOW ______
20. NESWESPALPEOR ______
21. STROGLETAHERS ______
22. ROMOSTRNAINTG ______
23. WATORDKABLYN ______
24. ROSUNTBSINDLE ______
25. WASTICHYOBUR ______
26. SHORUNSTFEWR ______

1 credit for each correct word!   **Credits:** ______

A 2 Where are the vowels?

In these sentences, all the vowels (a, e, i, o, u, y, ie, ea, ...) are missing. Fill them in and write down the sentences about Johnny and Timmy.

1. Wh s Jhnn sttng n th flr n hs rm nd lkng ndr th bd?

2. H hs gt _ nc nw schl nfrm fr hs cmprhnsv schl.

3. Bt h cn't fnd hs trsrs. N, th rn't ndr hs bd.

4. Nw h's gng nt Tmm's bdrm. Tmm s Jhnn's smll brthr.

5. Tmm sn't thr. H's plng crds wth th ct tsd.

6. Tht's nt s, bcs th ct s tng th crds.

7. Lk, nw _ cn s Jhnn gn. h, Jhnn, _ cnnt g t schl n Tmm's trsrs.
   Th r t smll!

This is not a labyrinth. It is a long chain of nouns. The last letter of one word is the first letter of the next word.

Go on. How many words can you find? Form a circle round the first / last letter of each noun.

Work with a partner. There is a credit for each word you know. Then it's your partner's turn. You also get a credit when your partner can't find a new word. Then you may go on.

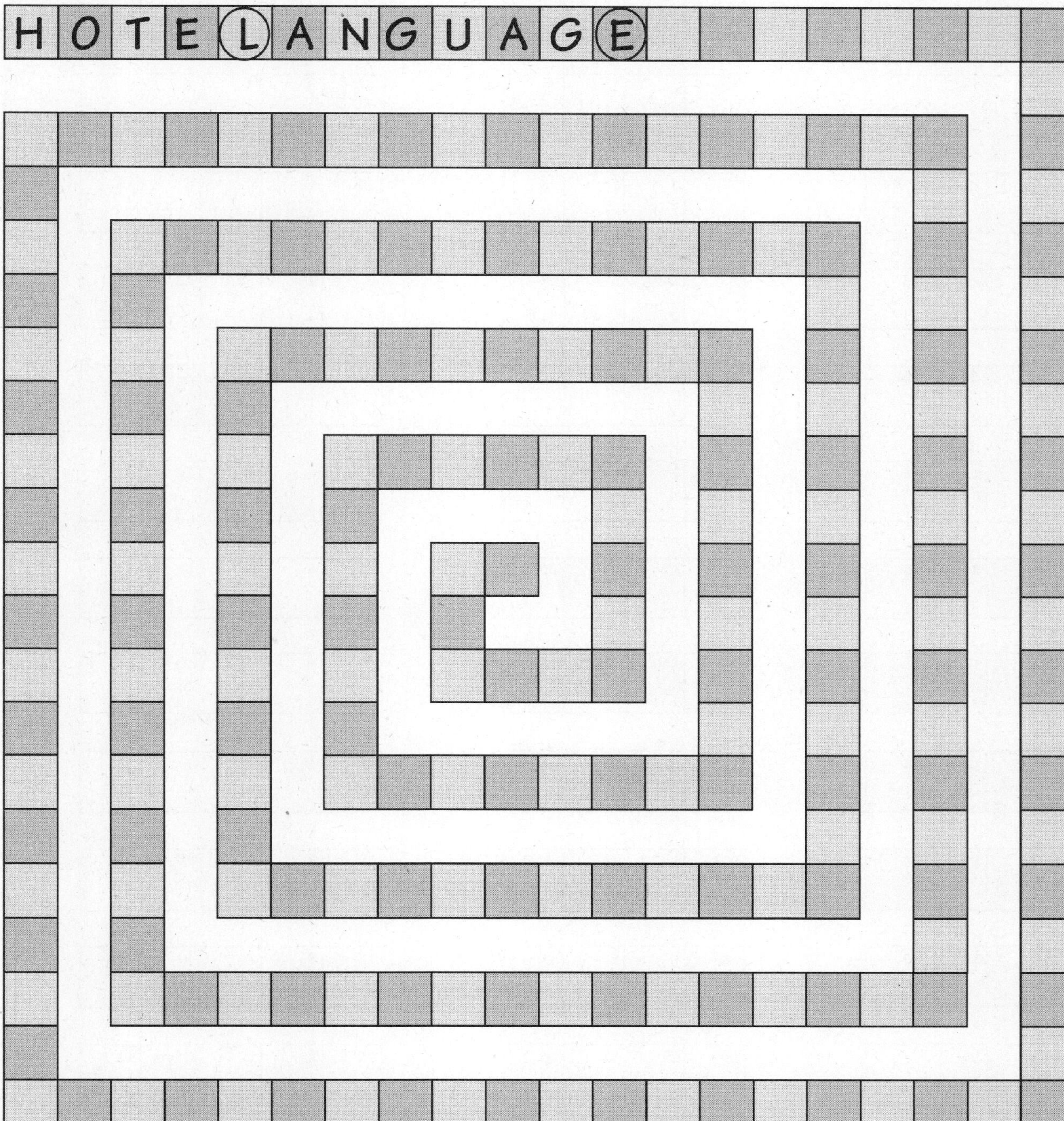

Can you read the word chain very fast?

Credits partner 1: ____________ **Credits partner 2:** ____________

 Letters and numbers

Write letters for the numbers in the boxes. Who can find all the words first?

a	b	c	d	e	f	g	h	i	j	k	l	m	n	o	p	q	r	s	t	u	v	w	x	y	z
1	2	3	4	5	6	7	8	9	10	11	12	13	14	15	16	17	18	19	20	21	22	23	24	25	26

1 a · 19 s · 11 k	6 · 1 · 3 · 5	14 · 5 · 22 · 5 · 18
4 · 1 · 4	19 · 1 · 13 · 5	16 · 9 · 5 · 3 · 5
10 · 15 · 2	14 · 5 · 24 · 20	20 · 18 · 1 · 9 · 14
20 · 23 · 15	2 · 1 · 2 · 25	5 · 1 · 18 · 12 · 25
7 · 5 · 20	20 · 9 · 13 · 5	16 · 1 · 16 · 5 · 18
4 · 1 · 25	19 · 8 · 15 · 23	3 · 8 · 9 · 12 · 4
16 · 5 · 20	13 · 21 · 19 · 20	20 · 8 · 18 · 5 · 5
8 · 15 · 23	2 · 9 · 11 · 5	19 · 8 · 15 · 21 · 20
6 · 12 · 25	16 · 12 · 1 · 14	23 · 1 · 20 · 5 · 18
22 · 1 · 14	8 · 1 · 12 · 6	20 · 8 · 9 · 14 · 7
2 · 21 · 19	11 · 9 · 20 · 5	14 · 9 · 7 · 8 · 20
4 · 15 · 7	19 · 15 · 15 · 14	18 · 21 · 12 · 5 · 18
2 · 21 · 20	20 · 8 · 9 · 19	23 · 15 · 13 · 5 · 14
15 · 21 · 18	8 · 15 · 21 · 18	12 · 21 · 3 · 11 · 25

1 credit for each correct word! **Credits:** ________

The letters of these words have been mixed up. Change their order, so that they make sense again.

1. at-o-m-h-b-r-o ____________

2. up-o-c-ar-b-d ____________

3. er-as-p-g-s-en ____________

4. i-ed-y-mm-i-el-at ____________

5. n-or-m-g-in ____________

6. y-il-a-r-wa ____________

7. rf-o-l-nd-u-w-e ____________

8. el-h-ep-t-ne-o ____________

9. pl-ea-n-e-pi-p ____________

10. on-at-i-t-i-nv-i ____________

11. om-c-w-e-el ____________

12. an-m-km-l-i ____________

13. er-g-nt-i-ti-es-n ____________

14. sp-w-pe-e-a-r-n ____________

15. co-o-at-h-e-l-c ____________

16. og-i-e-al-u-d ____________

17. s-er-s-tr-ou ____________

18. ig-u-e-bo-n-r-h ____________

19. at-l-m-p-or-f ____________

20. te-o-p-do-s-r ____________

21. al-u-y-us-l ____________

22. h-an-w-s-ic-d ____________

23. w-or-t-o-om-r ____________

24. be-y-t-r-rr-aw-s ____________

25. y-ob-n-d-o ____________

26. ne-z-a-ag-i-m ____________

27. y-el-o-v-l ____________

28. hu-et-p-c-k ____________

29. as-k-b-t-re-a-f ____________

30. le-am-x-e-p ____________

31. ic-if-t-d-l-u-f ____________

32. al-o-ot-l-f-b ____________

33. l-y-id-a-ho ____________

34. it-x-g-e-in-c ____________

35. as-p-c-en-e-il-c ____________

36. an-t-er-d-d-un-s ____________

37. in-v-en-g-e ____________

38. he-o-r-et-g-t ____________

39. ur-t-c-pi-e ____________

40. e-o-by-d-go ____________

1 credit for each correct word! **Credits:** ________

A 6 Across / down

1. *How many words can you find in this box?*
Write them down and count them. There are words "across" (→) and "down" (↓).

Example: **across**
1 sit, …

	1	2	3	4	5	6	7	8	9	10	11	12	13	14	15	16	17	18
1	F	S	I	T	W	O	N	F	C	A	R	U	S	T	O	D	A	Y
2	C	A	N	T	A	L	K	I	N	G	A	N	O	C	R	A	I	C
3	A	T	T	A	N	D	R	V	A	N	I	D	O	O	R	N	R	O
4	R	U	O	K	T	E	S	E	A	T	N	E	D	M	U	C	B	A
5	R	R	D	E	I	G	H	T	W	A	Y	R	R	I	B	E	S	T
6	Y	D	I	S	F	O	S	H	O	U	S	E	I	N	B	O	Y	G
7	I	A	R	B	L	I	S	I	M	S	L	O	N	G	E	A	S	Y
8	N	Y	T	O	O	N	O	M	A	K	E	T	K	E	R	W	T	Q
9	G	O	Y	X	O	G	O	T	N	I	E	V	E	R	Y	A	O	E
10	C	H	A	I	R	T	N	A	M	E	P	U	S	H	Q	Y	R	N
11	H	E	A	D	V	I	M	M	E	D	I	A	T	E	L	Y	Y	N
12	C	L	E	A	N	I	N	G	T	O	Y	M	A	H	F	R	E	E
13	A	L	L	R	E	P	A	I	R	U	A	F	T	E	R	B	L	W
14	N	O	T	K	I	C	K	R	I	B	R	A	I	A	I	H	A	S
15	B	R	I	D	G	E	E	L	C	L	E	C	O	V	E	R	U	P
16	A	A	M	T	H	E	Y	B	K	E	H	E	N	Y	N	T	G	A
17	C	D	E	F	B	R	E	A	K	F	A	S	T	G	D	S	H	P
18	K	I	B	R	O	T	H	E	R	T	O	D	L	I	T	T	L	E
19	D	O	G	P	U	L	L	O	V	E	R	W	X	V	U	O	U	R
20	O	F	G	E	R	M	A	N	P	F	R	O	M	E	S	P	E	N

1 credit for each correct word! **Credits:** ________

2. *Now make up a new puzzle for your neighbours. Work in groups of two or three. Use the alphabetical word list in your English book. (It is more difficult to find the* ***short*** *words!) Each group gives its puzzle to another group which has to find the words.*

	1	2	3	4	5	6	7	8	9	10	11	12	13	14	15	16	17	18
1																		
2																		
3																		
4																		
5																		
6																		
7																		
8																		
9																		
10																		
11																		
12																		
13																		
14																		
15																		
16																		
17																		
18																		
19																		
20																		

1 credit for each correct word! **Credits:** ________

You want to visit a friend who lives in England, so you're putting things in your suitcase. What have you already got in it?

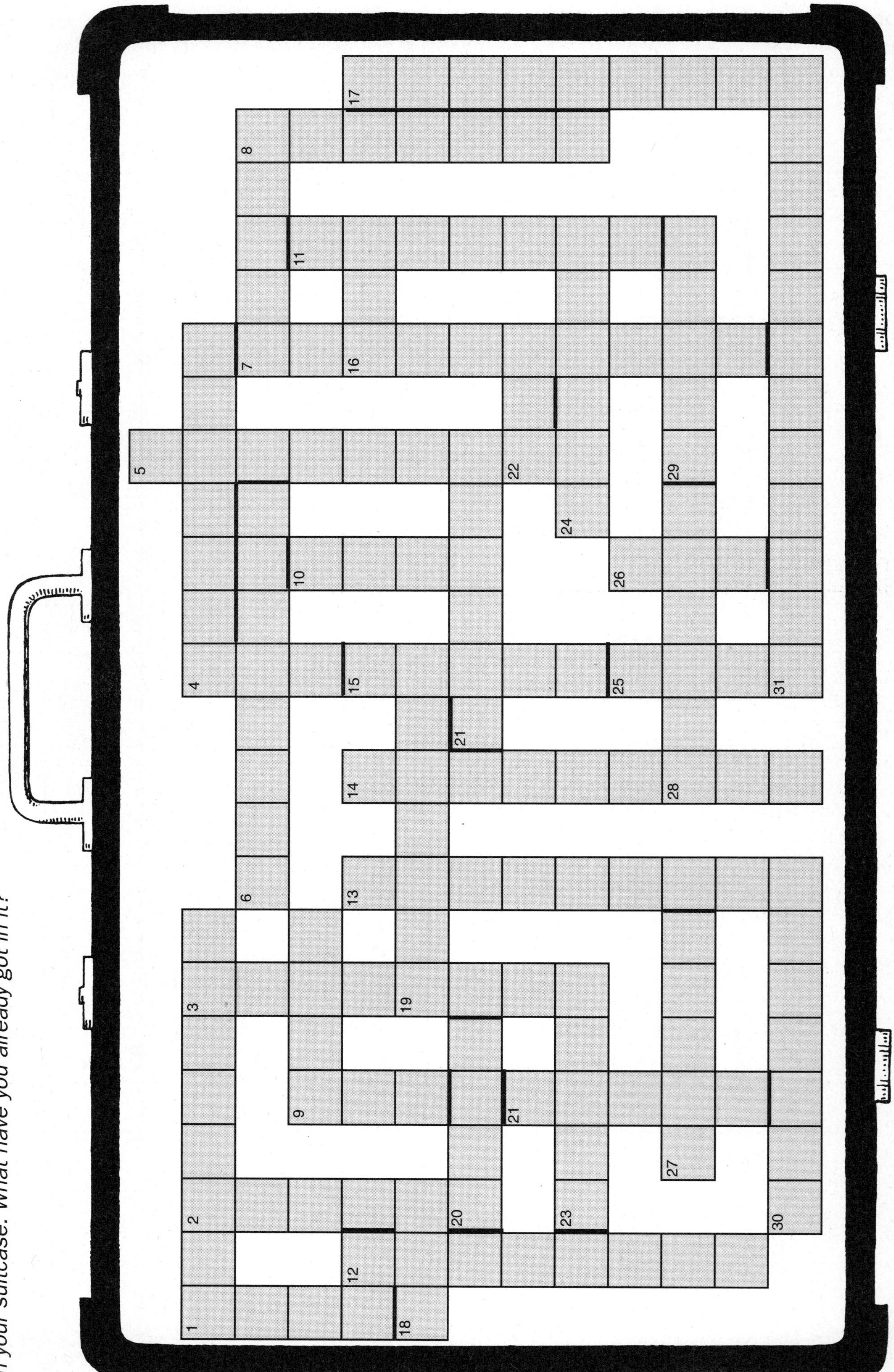

across:

1. Good idea; you can eat them on the train.
4. Why that? You can eat that, too, but you eat it with chips!
6. You need it when it rains.
7. Nobody can see them, but you can have a lot of good … in your head.
9. You can read it.
16. Yes, but I hope it is a toy … and not very big!
18. When the sun is shining, you can wear it on your head.
19. It is good when you're hungry, and you want something to eat that isn't sweet.
20. For your feet.
21. Yes, you can take photos with it.
22. This is not necessary: there's a lot of it in England. The English like drinking it.
23. You can't go to the city without … on your feet.
24. You can send it home when you're in England.
27. He's very nice. Does he want to come with you?
28. You can put it on when it's cold.
29. Why are you taking a … with you? It will make everyone afraid!
30. Yes, they look elegant, and you can wear them when the weather is not so warm.
31. Oh no! They taste nice and are sweet, but in your suitcase they can make all your clothes red!

down:

1. Yes, you can write a letter with it.
2. You can wear them, together with 3.
3. You can wear them, together with 2.
4. Good. You need it to open the door to your flat when you come back.
5. Tastes brown and sweet.
7. Your friend writes you a letter that you can come to see him.
8. They have got many colours; you can wear them with your jacket or pullover when it's cold.
9. What have you got in it? Sweets? A present?
10. Good idea. You can play it with your friends.
11. Why have you got that in your suitcase? Are you a policeman? Or do you want to wear it at school in England?
12. You must show it when you arrive in England.
13. Everybody wears them. They are warm.
14. Or you can wear these. You can open them.
15. Something else to wear. Everbody wears them, they often are blue.
17. Yes, your friend and you can listen to them.
21. You need it to pay for things.
25. You use them to play with.
26. You can find your way with it.

1 credit for each correct word! **Credits:** ________

A 8 Vowel mix

All these words have got four or more vowels (a, e, i, o, u). But the vowels are in the wrong order. Correct the words.

1. migezana — magazine
2. asylluu
3. etsoudi
4. ammydetilei
5. chaceloto
6. butuafiel
7. donong-riim
8. eundorgrund
9. jembla selu
10. greongrecer's
11. beifroynd
12. entiristeng
13. oftarneon
14. Medaumu Tassad's
15. striewbarres
16. witor-pastel
17. satcesiu
18. yvorebyde
19. eystayrde
20. pincal cese
21. racerd-pleyor
22. anviotitin
23. thi Styta ef Leuberto
24. panepplie
25. separmerkut
26. tixe dravir
27. skotebaard
28. cessotte-racerder

1 credit for each correct word! **Credits:** ________

Can you find out what the story is about? Write down the correct story.

⊞ = *a* ⅄ = *e* ◎ = *i* ☺ = *o* ✳ = *u* ✡ = *y*

Th⅄ K◎ss

D◎ck l◎v⅄d ◎n ☺xf☺rd, ⊞nd h⅄ h⊞d ⊞ n⅄w g◎rlfr◎⅄nd. H⅄r n⊞m⅄ w⊞s D⊞◎s✡, ⊞nd D◎ck l◎k⅄d h⅄r v⅄r✡ m✳ch. ☺n⅄ S✳nd⊞✡ th⅄✡ w⅄nt for ⊞ p◎cn◎c ◎n th⅄ c☺✳ntr✡, ⊞nd wh⅄n th⅄✡ w⅄r⅄ w⊞lk◎ng t☺ ⊞ n◎c⅄ pl⊞c⅄ n⅄⊞r ⊞ r◎v⅄r, th⅄✡ s⊞w ⊞ c☺w cl⅄⊞n◎ng ◎ts c⊞lf.

'L☺☺k, D⊞◎s✡,' D◎ck s⊞◎d, 'th⊞t c☺w's g◎v◎ng ◎ts c⊞lf ⊞ k◎ss. ◎sn't th⊞t n◎c⅄?'

D⊞◎s✡ st☺pp⅄d ⊞nd l☺☺k⅄d. Th⅄n sh⅄ sm◎l⅄d ⊞nd s⊞◎d, '✡⅄s, ◎t ◎s, D◎ck. ◎t's v⅄r✡ pr⅄tt✡.'

'D☺⅄sn't ◎t m⊞k⅄ y☺✳ w⊞nt t☺ h⊞v⅄ ⊞ k◎ss, t☺☺, D⊞◎s✡?' D◎ck s⊞◎d th⅄n, l☺☺k◎ng ⊞t h⅄r.

D⊞◎s✡ th☺✳ght f☺r ⊞ f⅄w s⅄c☺nds ⊞nd th⅄n sh⅄ s⊞◎d, sm◎l◎ng, 'N☺, ◎t d☺⅄sn't r⅄⊞ll✡, D◎ck. D☺⅄s ◎t m⊞k⅄ y☺✳ w⊞nt to h⊞v⅄ ☺n⅄?'

'✡⅄s, ◎t d☺⅄s, D⊞◎s✡,' D◎ck ⊞nsw⅄r⅄d, h☺ld◎ng h⅄r h⊞nd.

'⊞ll r◎ght, th⅄n g☺ ⊞nd g⅄t ⊞ k◎ss,' D⊞◎s✡ ⊞nsw⅄r⅄d, '⊞nd ◎'ll w⊞◎t h⅄r⅄. ◎t l☺☺ks l◎k⅄ ⊞ n◎c⅄, qu◎⅄t c☺w.'

A 10 What's the opposite?

Words like 'big' and 'small' are opposites.
Find 30 opposites here and mark them.

1.	behind	before	into	after
2.	play	dream	pay	work
3.	come in	fall down	get lost	go out
4.	laugh	cry	shout	like
5.	on time	on foot	at once	by plane
6.	bring	repair	take	see
7.	everyone	someone	who	nobody
8.	sun	wind	summer	rain
9.	take off	put on	wear	carry
10.	hate	like	love	cry
11.	trousers	tie	skirt	coat
12.	blue	white	green	black
13.	long	tall	round	short
14.	nice	new	sure	old
15.	clean	nice	dirty	bad
16.	boring	funny	silly	ready
17.	under	between	over	onto
18.	sentence	shout	answer	question
19.	Thank you	You're welcome	How are you?	Hello
20.	where	why	who	because
21.	wrong	right	straight	all right
22.	person	house	thing	dog
23.	boy	mother	girl	grandfather
24.	sometimes	always	never	often
25.	take turns	go on	move	stop
26.	get	have	find	lose
27.	must	may	want	don't
28.	up	right	over	left
29.	useful	different	same	clear
30.	aunt	friend	uncle	neighbour

1 credit for a correct solution! **Credits:** ______

A lot of adjectives are hiding here.
Mark them. How many can you find?

kenfpsysezuexcitinggktindfegreenlfjerybvlkzoquietzsedfokgteasylophjodly
stfeinterestingoklpnhelkfifullpoltunbvebluvfelovelyonmhurfcsepiousilbade
openlofrebvjioplpillomkzedrtubornvocarefulluckypolnutrefreemondinsolda
ntilyesedolittlepertoftikoranewamitrousyfnicelontkwecoldlecopdunidifficult
epludikatefarostiflumetgreatoquantopluxangrywortabixondilincleverleova
ngtedrfinerintiplonxwancouprinctingocleanavitiocouliemptyloaferpluchighi
ngrousgoodethelixbertuntronicreadyoftringrkopdjexgamkintershappyonks
deohtvecdrenkousoldifferentingplindpzejsbawlquallyembluermestingloust
ernimpinunhappyaoestirnatiornaltrumpouspskrneilquomxcshortoftontimro
uslymatroxwrongingastenmkefrobtuchinkunxquastrongilyngesiblourmihrf
waplmossecretorgawonnyalwarmaprotiblankingofrousytrifunnyhenderplui
mtrivioundifoustrexactincturiplousivityusibkfdwxhzuolpusefulchirblamertm
inkrtelgofredloppyblearlyantishunitytypicaltransousyedifingklaribgedrousk
gedxousurprisedorlyfgwanslgzbrownojumfrumingaarfyokmalderoterribleo
ndrynalotbdwonderfulagrcditrawontilygreyungpkerdousvimnertincheavyol
krecgfesaoilkpmblackoptrionalflortruerinkinglouslyominontalrealwertorale
martinglonyarrightoklerdwxbcepmihztousullexpensiveunoodeyirtousjtecfr
cnervousurbvfseolukmnjiofrtelnjipyontriangulingadirtybigdarkastoulygrzbk
sewrspooryhuntrixingefterlingheffalumpyarisosbeautifulonhrteaslomsedri
ngalbicoufrofantasticourengkuofglionfgespastingondulwominglyorshorsel
ingofamousclartphwsuntonousnelourcrazyfulflurunnywonningarouliousyto

1 credit for each correct word! **Credits:** ________

railway
mice
key
to turn left
straight on
page
What's the matter?
really
of course
spoon
forest
at the top of

cannot
never
biology
him
language
castle
rabbit
friend
tomato ketchup
autumn
group
glad

for
by train
entrance
excuse me!
to look up
not
to shout
those
to turn off
purse
men
to use

near
outdoor swimming-pool
to be over
plastic
to be lucky
to rescue
game
kitchen
medicine
for example
soon
most

they
leg
anybody
bridge
certain
anywhere
green
to touch
up
floor
expensive
until

to want
museum
other
my
unhappy
to ride
just a minute
sweets
upstairs
to wear
thief
wet

Credits: ____________________

Credits: ____________________

Regeln für die Klasse:

1. Please form pairs.
2. Every pupil will get a list of words or expressions. Do not show your list to your partner.
3. First you must try to explain one of your expressions to your partner.
   Start with any word or expression. Then your partner explains one of her/his expressions to you.
4. But be careful: you may not use any German, you may not act or show anything.
5. If your partner guesses your expression and can say it in English, he scores a credit. If you use German vocabulary, gestures or anything that is not English, he/she scores another credit. You have got thirty seconds to explain each word.
6. Some words are more difficult to explain than others; but these words are also more difficult to guess!
7. When the teacher ends the game, count your credits.

Have fun!

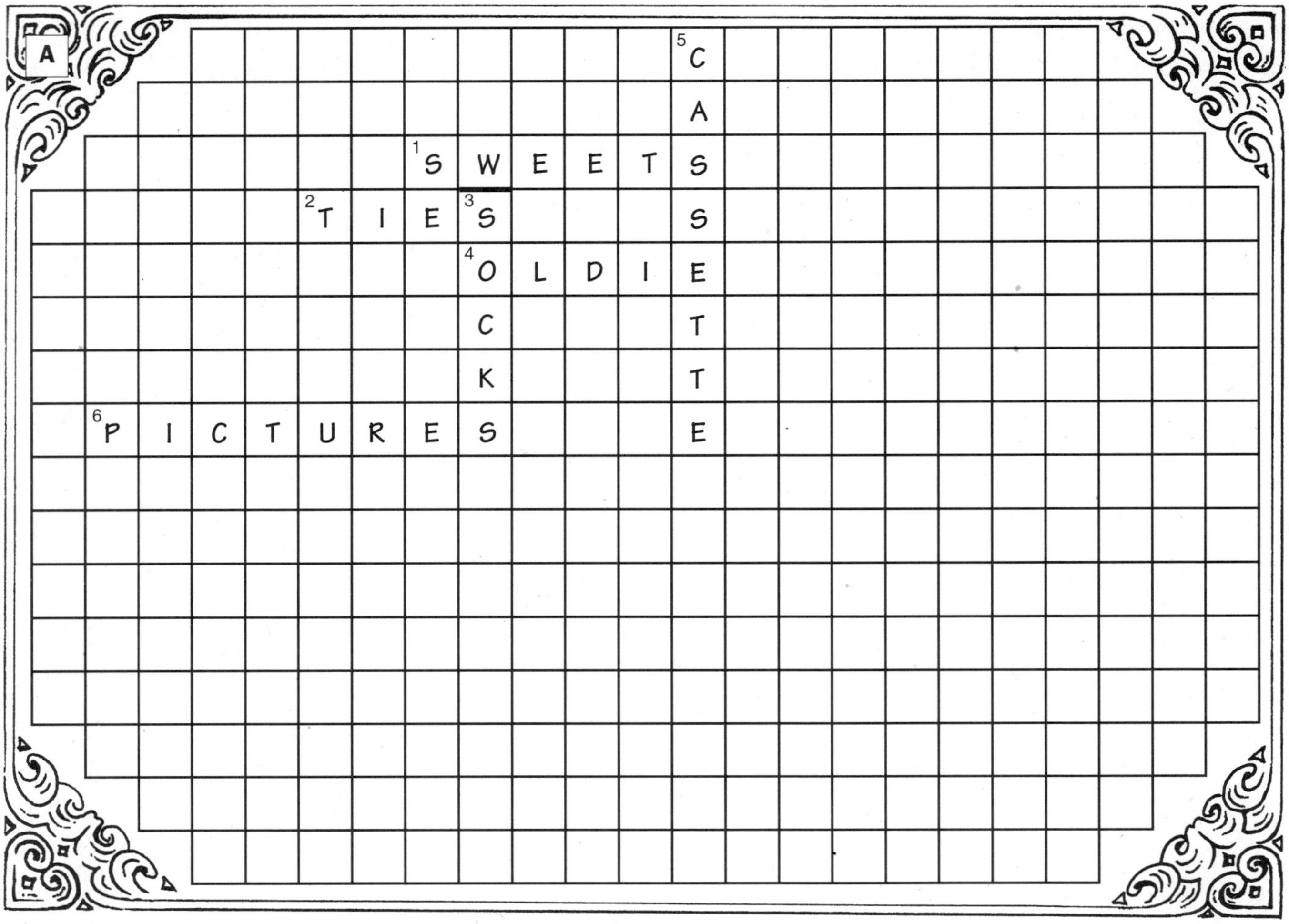
A
1 SWEETS
2 TIES
3 SOCKS
4 OLDIE
5 CASSETTE
6 PICTURES

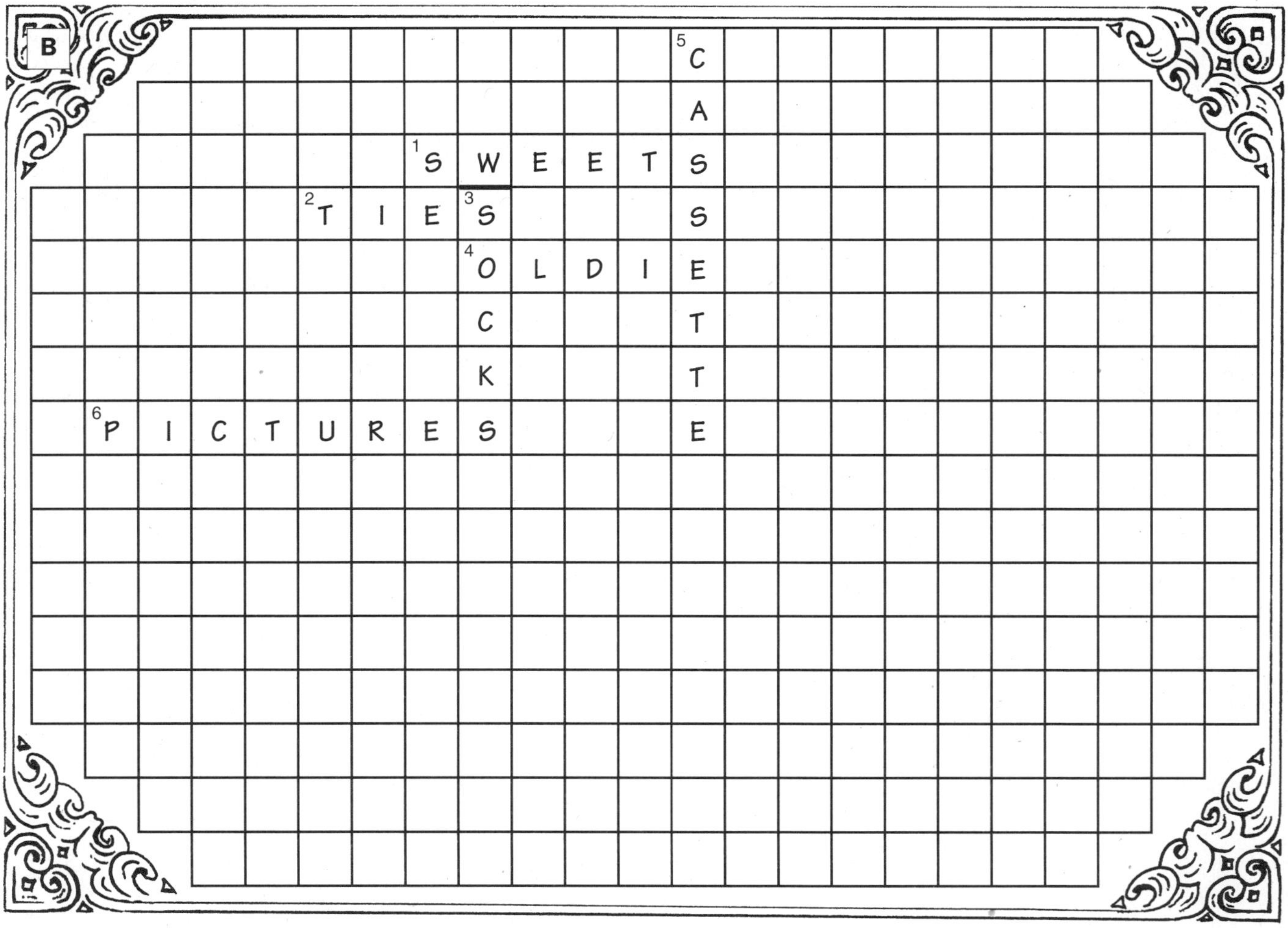
B
1 SWEETS
2 TIES
3 SOCKS
4 OLDIE
5 CASSETTE
6 PICTURES

Regeln für die Klasse:

This is a present for someone else in the class.
You decide what you want to put into the box (for example sweets, ideas, and ...).

1. Find words to fill the crossword puzzle in box A. You can open your English book to look for words.
2. Each word in your puzzle gets a number and an explanation like in the example below. Write the explanations down on a separate sheet.
3. When you have finished your crossword puzzle, give your explanations to somebody else in the class. Choose anyone you like. He or she must then find out which presents you have put into the parcel.
   She/he can write them down in box B.

Example:

across
1. They are bad for your teeth.
2. Businessmen wear them.
4. Your parents don't listen to techno, they prefer an ... .

down
3. You wear them on your feet.
5. If you don't listen to the radio, maybe you listen to a ... .

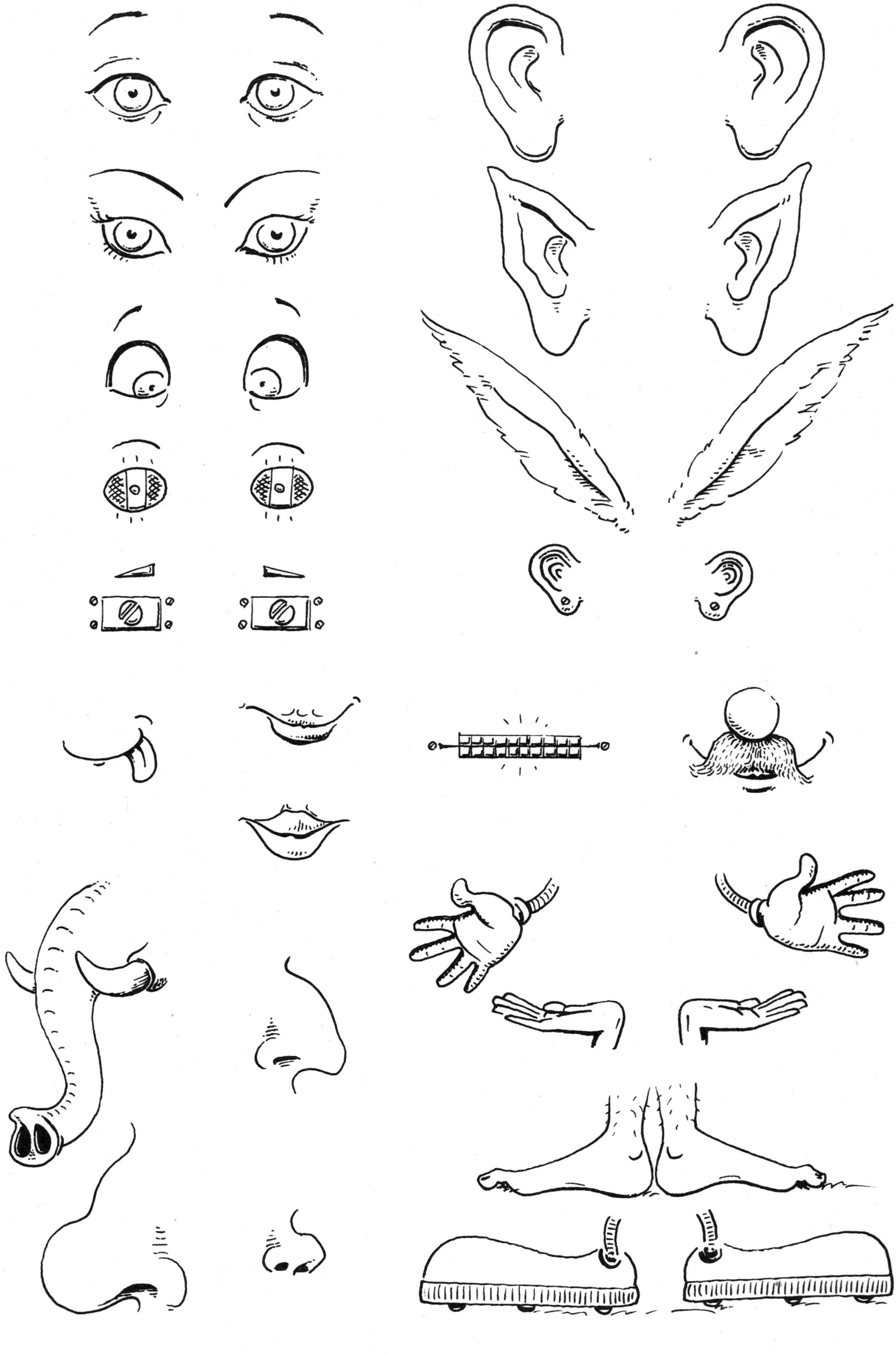

Regeln für die Klasse:

You need scissors and glue to play the game.

1. Draw your own robot on a separate sheet of paper. Here are some ideas you can use. Cut the parts you need with your scissors and stick them onto your piece of paper.
2. Do you like your robot? Now take your picture and an empty piece of paper, and find a partner. You may sit where you like, even on the floor.
3. Your partner must try to draw your robot, and you must try to draw her/his robot.Tell her/him in English what your robot looks like. First you tell her/him a detail, then it's your partner's turn.
4. Then look at each other's pictures. How correct are they? Do they look funny?

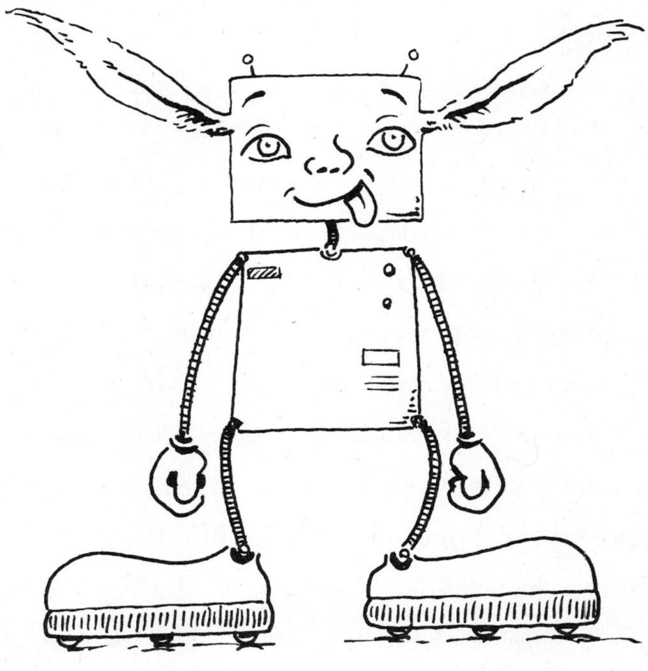

A 15 Headings

Find the four words in the wordbox which go together.
In each group, there are three words and one heading

1. concert ____ to sing, to listen, instrument ____
2. ____ ____
3. ____ ____
4. ____ ____
5. ____ ____
6. ____ ____
7. ____ ____
8. ____ ____
9. ____ ____
10. ____ ____
11. ____ ____
12. ____ ____
13. ____ ____
14. ____ ____
15. ____ ____
16. ____ ____
17. ____ ____
18. ____ ____
19. ____ ____
20. ____ ____

to arrest ★ waiter ★ language ★ pullover ★ son ★ school ★ meal ★ Greek burglar ★ lunch ★ ~~to sing~~ ★ Buckingham Palace ★ ambulance ★ hot ★ green seat ★ settlers ★ Robin Hood ★ red and white scarf ★ late ★ post office Plymouth Harbour ★ lesson ★ Italian ★ clothes ★ Little Italy ★ family Davy Crocket ★ pence ★ summer ★ ~~to listen~~ ★ stretcher ★ stamp ★ the Thames hour ★ breakfast ★ the Pilgrims ★ shirt ★ Madison Square Garden ★ money orange ★ first aid ★ ~~concert~~ ★ restaurant ★ folk hero ★ London ★ trumpet sunshine ★ Central Park ★ time ★ letter ★ dollar ★ teacher ★ aunt ★ Liverpool fan ★ police ★ Buffalo Bill ★ flowers ★ Spanish ★ New York ★ the Mayflower badge ★ trousers ★ dinner ★ Big Ben ★ yellow ★ eight o'clock ★ to send ★ table homework ★ injured ★ thief ★ pound ★ sister ★ ~~instrument~~ ★ colour

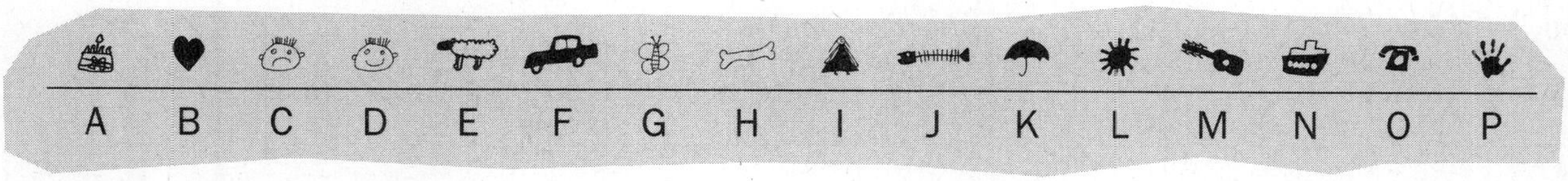

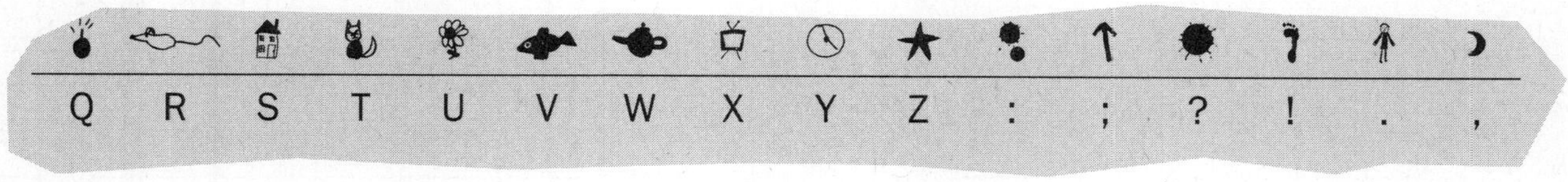

This is a letter in a secret code. Can you find out what it is about?

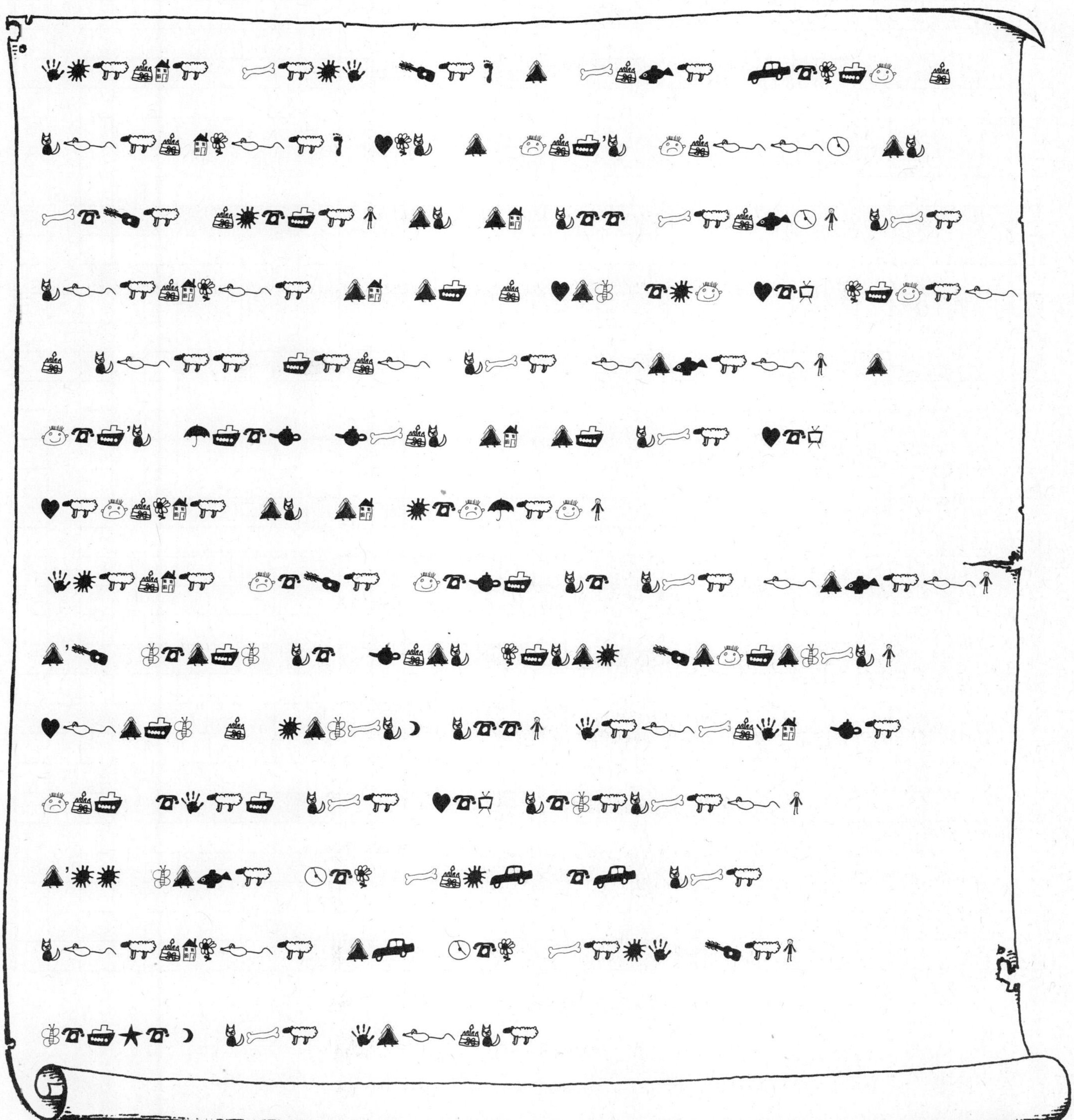

The next day you want to tell your friend about the adventure. Write a letter to her/him. Of course you're going to write the letter in the secret code, so that nobody else can read it.

A 17 Connecting words

Fill in words (names of countries, food names or people's professions).

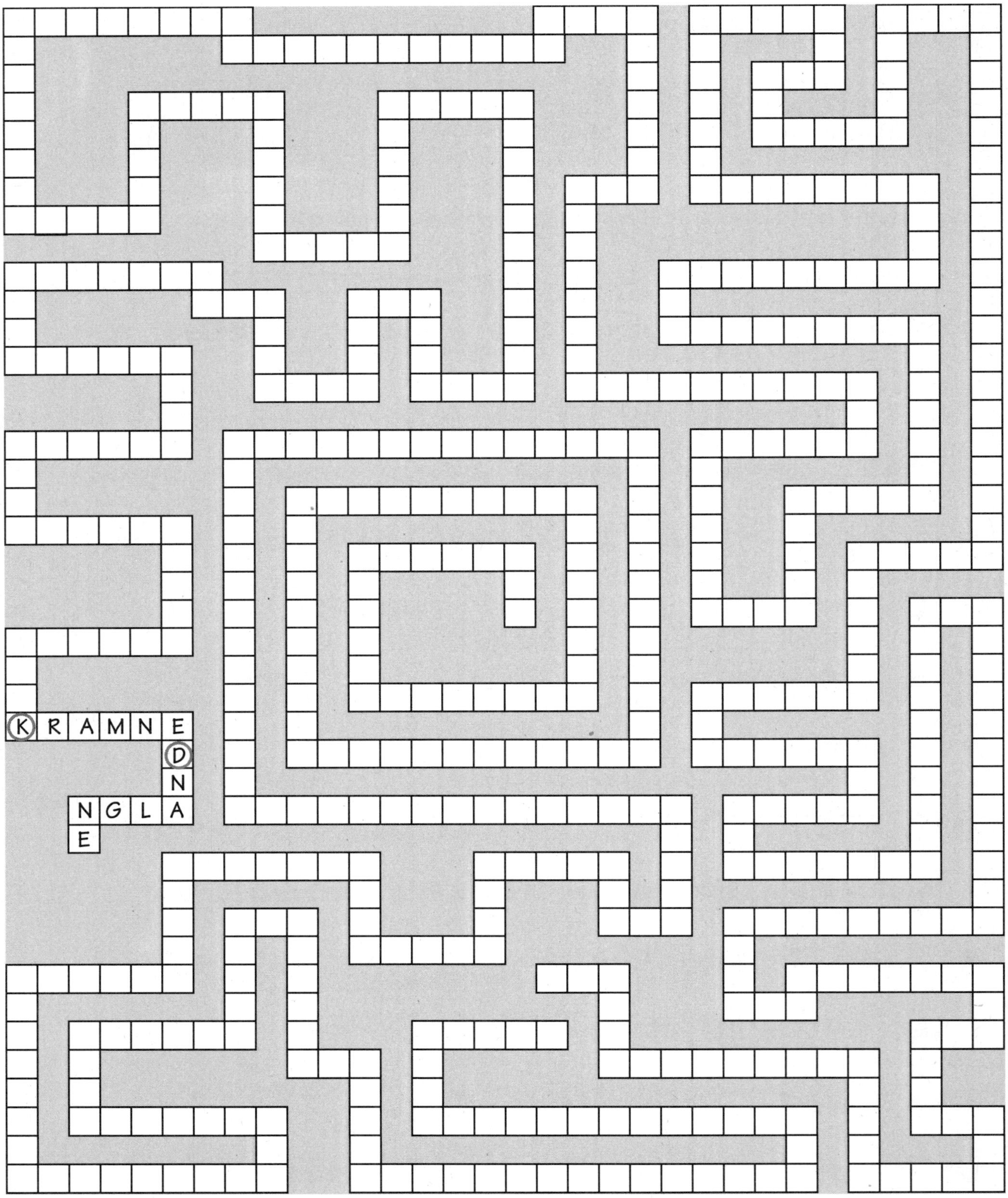

countries: ________ **words** **1 credit for each correct word!**

food: ________ **words** **Credits:** ________

professions: ________ **words**

The following story tells us about one of Robin Hood's adventures.
But only the fragments in box I are in the correct order.
Find the story and write it down.

I	II	III
1. All the people	arrived	it was Robin Hood.
2. There were sports and games,	asked the King, after	against each other,
3. Now the King and the queen	of the group	in Lincoln green.
4. The groups	they disappeared	he had given away the prizes.
5. but in the final round	were now standing everywhere	would be left.
6. Everybody was excited,	in and around Nottingham	and in the end they won all the prizes.
7. But nobody knew	had to shoot	to arrest the outlaws,
8. The King's men shot well,	the six men who where dressed	at the field.
9. "Who are you?"	and later the King's best bowmen	took off his hood,
10. Suddenly the first man	and everybody wore the colours	into the forest.
11. and there was a cry of surprise	but these men shot better,	came to the tourney.
12. The King	in the field:	with their bows and arrows ready.
13. but Robin Hood's men	only the winners	would shoot for prizes.
14. Silently,	ordered his guards	of their favourite bowmen.

2 credits for each correct line! **Credits:** ________

Samuel Morse made this alphabet known to the public in 1837:

•—	a	•—•	r	———••	8
—•••	b	•••	s	————•	9
—•—•	c	—	t	—————	0
—••	d	••—	u	••••••	.
•	e	•••—	v	—•—•—•	;
••—•	f	•——	w	———•••	:
——•	g	—••—	x	••——••	?
••••	h	—•——	y	——••——	!
••	i	——••	z	—••••—	hyphen
•———	j	————	ch	•————•	apostrophy
—•—	k	•————	1	—•——•—	bracket
•—••	l	••———	2	•—••—•	inverted commas
——	m	•••——	3	••——•—	underline
—•	n	••••—	4	•—•—•••	new line
———	o	•••••	5		
•——•	p	—••••	6		
——•—	q	——•••	7		

Translate these words. They tell you names of animals.

1. —•—•/•—/—// __________
2. •/•—/——•/•—••/•// __________
3. •—•/•—/—•••/—•••/••/—// __________
4. ••••/•/—••/——•/•/••••/———/——•// __________
5. ••—•/••/•••/••••// __________
6. ——•/———/———/•••/•// __________
7. •••/—•/•—/—•—/•// __________
8. —•••/••/•—•/—••// __________
9. •••/•——•/••/—••/•/•—•// __________
10. •••/••••/•/•/•——•// __________

Can you write some short English sentences in Morse writing? Try to use names of animals. Give your sentences to your neighbour and ask him/her to read them.

*One of the four words in each line doesn't really fit in.
It shouldn't be there. Mark every "odd man".*

A

1.	exact	correct	right	important
2.	bad	boring	clean	negative
3.	lend	win	get	find
4.	sore	worried	hurt	swollen
5.	interesting	wonderful	excellent	super
6.	creepy	terrible	cruel	frightening
7.	tall	high	gigantic	wide
8.	wetter	nearer	important	better
9.	complete	carry	transport	bring
10.	beautiful	great	lovely	pretty

B

1.	brush	wipe	wash	roll
2.	bark	whisper	roar	chirp
3.	walk	run	ride	jog
4.	shout	laugh	smile	grin
5.	break	tighten	fasten	bind
6.	learn	break	teach	know
7.	conquer	rob	fight	compare
8.	drown	shoot	arrest	kill
9.	drive	swim	ride	fly
10.	put up	examine	go on	give out

C

1.	nose	hand	eyes	mouth
2.	Sue	Peggie	Diana	Mark
3.	bird	eagle	budgie	blackbird
4.	orange	banana	carrot	apple
5.	London	Edinburgh	York	New York
6.	banjo	computer	guitar	piano
7.	garage	attic	bedroom	kitchen
8.	cake	present	invitation	school
9.	cheetah	lion	elephant	tiger
10.	bow	fun	arrow	shot

1 credit for each correct "odd man out"! **Credits: ________**

A 21 Bingo

Number Bingo

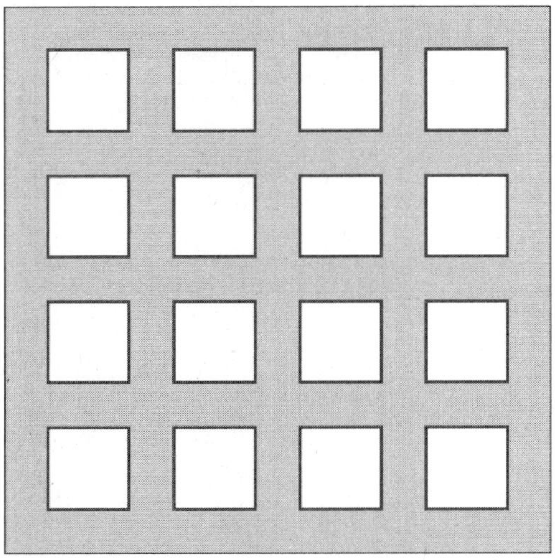

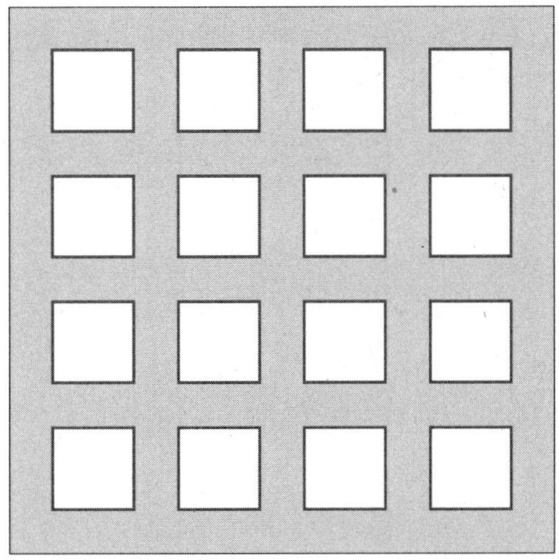

Word Bingo

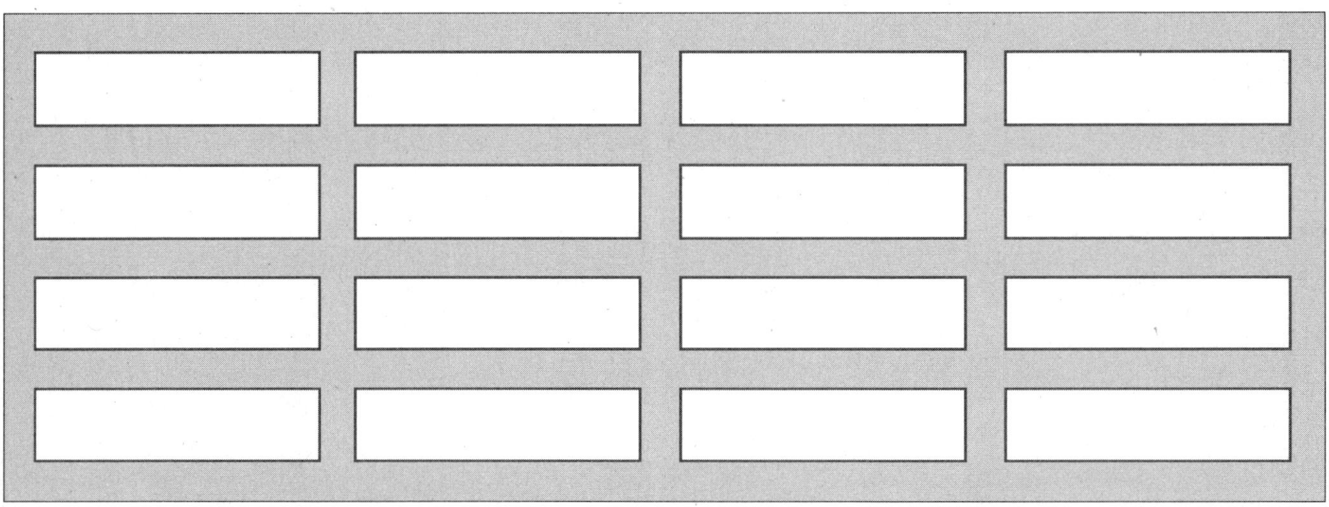

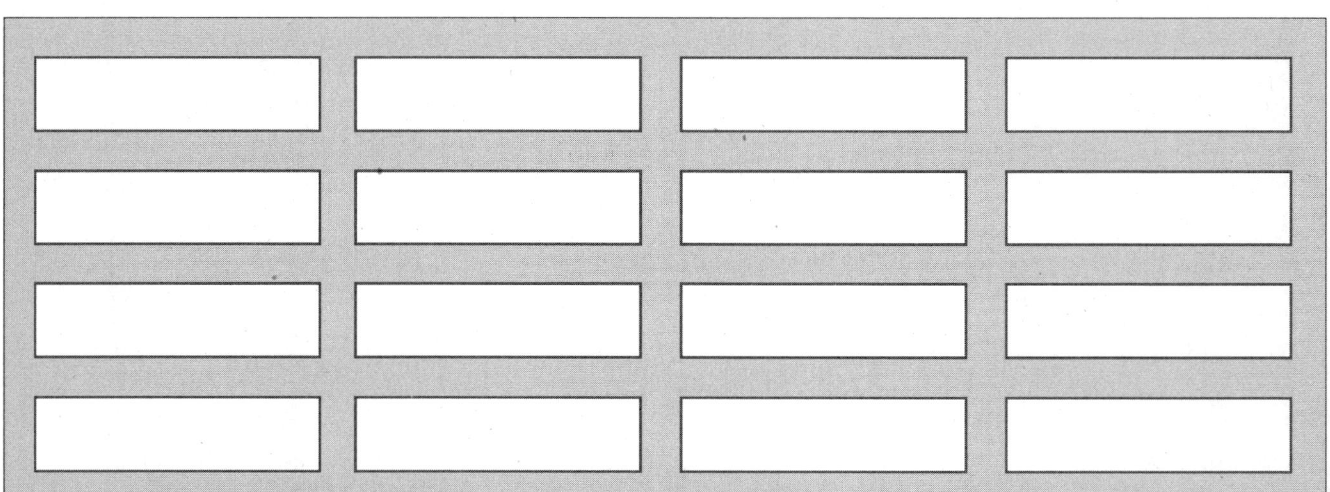

In these words prepositions and pronouns, nouns and verbs are hiding.
Find the words and write them down. You may not change the order of the letters.

	Prepositions/pronouns		Nouns		Verbs	
1.	floor	for	figure	fire	trumpet	met
2.	goodbye		proper		stewardess	
3.	office		timetable		rafting	
4.	the industry		stewardess		collecting	
5.	station		morning		safetey	
6.	those		husband		shadow	
7.	working		chocolate		Sherwood Forest	
8.	thunder		certain		blood pressure	
9.	money		language		comprehensive	
10.	drowning		change		supermarket	
11.	a father		carrot		yesterday	
12.	newspaper		hamster		woman	
13.	injection		police-station		morning	
14.	Christmas		prisoner		breakdance	
15.	shine		questionnaire		vegetables	
16.	happening		doctor		waitress	
17.	thunderstorm		cookery		swimming-pool	
18.	rushed		medicine		almost	
19.	cheerful		policeman		sweatshirt	
20.	Indian		worried		perhaps	
21.	smile		Great Britain		holiday	
22.	start		impossible		neighbour	
23.	wore		problem		camera	
24.	lists		dessert		almost	
25.	yoghurt		starving		headache	
26.	tourist		practice		lemonade	
27.	trumpet		present		football	
28.	the sky		interest		family	
29.	hitting		suddenly		east	
30.	shirts		pullover		caretaker	

1 credit for each word you find! **Credits:** ________

A 23 Captions

What are these people saying? Find captions.

aus: Rauschenbach, Erich: Cool bleiben ..., Oldenburg: Lappan Verlag 1990

Form new words with the letters of these words.
You mustn't change the order of the letters.
Write down the words you have found.

1. TIMETABLE meal, meet, able, (time, table)
2. FRIGHTENED
3. HELICOPTER
4. MILKSHAKE
5. LEMONADE
6. FORECAST
7. PREPOSITION
8. HAIRDRESSER
9. BREAKDANCE
10. BUFFALO BILL
11. ENTERTAINING
12. VEGETABLES
13. BLOOD PRESSURE
14. INTERESTING
15. SKATEBOARDING
16. TEMPERATURE
17. NORTHEAST
18. POCKET MONEY
19. CHARACTER
20. FOOTBALL
21. CORNFLAKES

Credits: 1 for words with three letters
2 for words with four letters
3 for words with five letters

Credits: ______

A 25 What a shock!

1. come in
   see
   be
   can

2. go
   find
   take
   run

3. put
   hit
   think
   tell

4. break
   fall
   have
   hear

5. stand
   hide
   become
   say

Regeln für die Klasse:

Form pairs or groups of three or four. Only one in each group can see the overhead, the others must sit with their backs to it.

1. Tell your partner the beginning of the story. Use the past tense of the verbs given.
2. Now let your partner(s) look at the picture, then change seats. Somebody else in the group can see the next picture now, and she/he goes on with the story. (Do not forget to use the verbs.)
3. Please turn round now, everybody, to see the last picture. Can we finish the story together?

Many English proverbs have been taken from the animal world.
Unfortunately, the proverbs on this page are all mixed up.
Can you solve the puzzle? Find the right proverbs and write them down.

The early	your own	they are hatched.
If you pay	bird	flock together
Don't kill	doesn't make	your bite.
Fine feathers	your chickens before	hunt with the hounds.
Don't foul	is worth	will play.
Birds	peanuts	in the mouth.
When the cat's	is worse than	you can't make it drink.
One swallow	make	the golden egg.
Don't count	of feather	two in the bush.
Your bark	an old dog	a summer.
Never look	dogs	new tricks.
You can't run	the goose that lays	lie.
A bird in the hand	away, the mice	fine birds.
You can't teach	to the water, but	nest.
You may take a horse	with the hare and	catches the worm.
Let sleeping	a gift horse	you get monkeys.

2 credits for each correct proverb! **Credits:** ________

1. Lieber den Spatz in der Hand als die Taube auf dem Dach.

2. Wenn die Katze aus dem Haus ist, tanzen die Mäuse.

3. Bellende Hunde beißen nicht.

4. Schlachte nicht die Henne, die goldene Eier legt.

5. Von nichts kommt nichts. / Wer nicht wagt, der nicht gewinnt.

6. Einem geschenkten Gaul sieht man nicht ins Maul.

7. Man kann nicht zwei Herren dienen.

8. Morgenstund hat Gold im Mund.

9. Was Hänschen nicht lernt, lernt Hans nimmermehr.

10. Man kann niemand zu seinem Glück zwingen.

11. Eine Schwalbe macht noch keinen Sommer.

12. Schlafende Hunde soll man nicht wecken.

13. Kleider machen Leute.

14. Beschmutze nicht dein eigenes Nest!

15. Man soll den Tag nicht vor dem Abend loben.

16. Gleich und gleich gesellt sich gern.

A 27 Intruders

In each line there are six words. Four of these words belong together, but two of them don't. Find these two and mark them.

1.	thin	happy	fat	tall	small	nice
2.	crazy	silly	fool	question	idiot	landing
3.	cold	cough	trainer	headache	speak	appendix
4.	listen	scream	speak	understand	talk	shout
5.	cardigan	bitter	trousers	blouse	tie	violet
6.	rose	sank	lily	violet	tulip	apple
7.	farm	hedgehog	fox	crocodile	zoo	elephant
8.	mile	big	litre	height	foot	yard
9.	boot	windscreen	taxi	headlight	gear	driver
10.	swan	wing	penguin	hen	feather	parrot
11.	prisoner	policewoman	justice	law	millionaire	lose
12.	meat	marmalade	chicken	eggs	toast	cornflakes
13.	sleep	break	yawn	see	dream	lie
14.	belly	finger	sugar	feet	knee	giant
15.	nervous	lonely	frightened	fear	horrible	afraid
16.	morning	second-hand	plant	shopping	buy	market
17.	apricot	fruit	strawberry	sweet	lemon	pineapple
18.	not at all	a lot	other	hardly	fairly	but
19.	paint	gallery	museum	statue	cinema	theatre
20.	can	may	want	must	has	needn't
21.	newspaper	scandal	magazine	advertisement	comic	book
22.	ambulance	accident	battery	emergency	first aid	entrance
23.	drive	handlebars	bicycle	bell	tank	ride
24.	cube	circle	triangle	three	square	horizontal
25.	under	back	on top	into	behind	above
26.	score	rocket	jog	match	lose	goal
27.	ship	caravan	tent	doll	hotel	camper
28.	stamp	guest	envelope	amuse	write	letter
29.	dice	board game	teddy	counter	bed	rule
30.	fitness	party	birthday	invite	present	suddenly

2 credits for each correct line! **Credits:** ________

Can you solve this letter puzzle?
Use the letters in brackets to find the hidden words.

1. eno (y,j) enjoy
2. dappeed (r,a,s,i) ________
3. cmcal (h,i,e) ________
4. amane (l,b,u,c) ________
5. uersod (t,d,o,n) ________
6. eion (s,c,i,d) ________
7. pend (a,x,i,p) ________
8. eoure (c,g,n,a) ________
9. fail (i,a,r,m) ________
10. endy (r,l,f,i) ________
11. irode (c,t,n,u) ________
12. poorapy (t,h,g,h) ________
13. atonity (i,l,a,n) ________
14. pulain (o,p,o,t) ________
15. haleg (l,e,n,c) ________
16. retar (c,e,y,s) ________
17. cares (s,l,e) ________
18. Haeen (w,l,o,l) ________
19. oouul (f,r,l,c) ________
20. dored (c,v,i) ________
21. centi (i,t,s,s) ________
22. andse (a,c,l,p) ________
23. ine (j,r,u) ________
24. linig (t,h,n,g) ________
25. saboo (r,k,p,c) ________
26. emin (l,r,t,a) ________
27. usan (b,h,d) ________
28. nead (t,i,s) ________
29. stom (s,c,u) ________
30. lar (y,e,w) ________
31. prad (u,e,e,s) ________
32. cenry (t,u) ________
33. queinnaie (t,r,s,o) ________
34. peale (i,p,n,p) ________
35. reare (e,s,h) ________
36. verrat (f,o,c,h) ________
37. seer (v,l,a) ________
38. verere (h,y,e,w) ________
39. unessan(m,b,i,s) ________
40. ugut (h,d,n,o) ________
41. rthquk (e,e,a,a) ________
42. seran (h,i,f,m) ________
43. bedane (k,c,r,a) ________
44. pecaly (s,i,e,l) ________
45. ilfind (r,r,g,e) ________
46. Epan (e,o,u,r) ________
47. loueaer (p,d,k,s) ________
48. miately (d,m,i,e) ________

1 credit for each correct word!

3 credits for being among the first 5 to finish the puzzle! **Credits:** ________

A 29 Quintet

In each of the boxes A, B and C, five expressions belong together. We call them a quintet. There are five quintets in each box. Find all the quintets and write down the solution with a headline of your own.

A

~~fish and chips~~ ★ policeman ★ why ★ concert ★ catch ★ afraid ★ player
how old ★ prison ★ ~~carrot~~ ★ nervous ★ listen ★ ~~vegetables~~ ★ where ★ piano
~~tea~~ ★ thief ★ happy ★ what ★ curious ★ jazz ★ ~~ham~~ ★ angry ★ steal ★ who

B

pig ★ Stetson hat ★ alarm bell ★ swimming-pool ★ Texas ★ degrees
siren ★ milking ★ holidays ★ cow herds ★ cloudy ★ rescue
thunderstorm ★ ice-cream ★ ride ★ farmhand ★ burn ★ fog ★ hen
sunglasses ★ fireman ★ campfire ★ lightning ★ feed ★ sea

C

coach ★ editor ★ Hollywood ★ sand ★ nurse ★ ad ★ visitor ★ wave
famous building ★ Silicon Valley ★ doctor ★ seagull ★ guide ★ news
giant redwoods ★ museum ★ fishing boats ★ operation ★ reporter
Gold Rush ★ camera ★ patient ★ dune ★ sports page ★ Death Valley

2 credits for each correct quintet! **Credits:** ______

A

1. **Food:** fish and chips, carrot, vegetables, tea, ham
2. ______
3. ______
4. ______
5. ______

B

1. ______
2. ______
3. ______
4. ______
5. ______

C

1. ______
2. ______
3. ______
4. ______
5. ______

A 30 Towns/countries

Towns	Countries	Actions (Verbs)	Animals	Adjectives	Food	Famous people	Credits

In each of these rows, a sentence is hiding. You can find it by crossing out letters in each word. Write down the sentences you've found.

1. Showel - fare - youth?
   How are you?
2. Letter - use - grow - brandy - training.
3. Chance - Israel - helicopter - youngster?
4. Then - rushed - tooth - deliver - bring - thunder - chemistry.
5. Whatever - died - Italy - secretary?
6. History - song - wanders - reloading.
7. Sheep – leaflet – hit – kind - other - caravan.
8. Wonder - stormy - waters - father - be still - soft - stall.
9. Theatre - we're - bewares - skin - mother - Black Forest.
10. Shame - painted - anthem - billion.
11. Misery - haunt - spent - mile - also - cared.
12. Danish - blinked - stalking - stove - shear.
13. Cancer - India - secret - their - roommate - nowhere?
14. What's - underground - therapy - east?

1 credit for each sentence! **Credits:** ________

noise loud traffic to shout	**tea** to drink English coffee	**saddle** horse to ride to sit	**Robin Hood** outlaw hero to rob
pence money to pay rich/poor	**hair** head long/short no colour	**customs** officer foreign country	**dish-washer** dirty clean water
cinema film story to watch	**clothes** to wear no clothes! e.g. pullover	**building** house high big	**bright** dark light to see
class pupil girl/boy to learn	**brown** colour to see hair	**chocolate** to eat sweet to like	**bridge** water river cross
temperature hot/warm/cold to show ill	**train** to go between fast	**statue** art to make famous	**surgery** doctor to help ill
name person to call people	**biscuits** packet sweet to taste	**news** to tell to happen interesting	**meal** to eat breakfast lunch

sky above high blue	**budgie** bird small to fly	**moment** short time minute	**shadow** dark to see person
the Channel England France between	**feet** two body walk	**entrance** to go in door out	**grandmother** old woman parents
forest tree a lot of to grow	**weather** cold/hot warm to tell	**maths** school to learn number	**thunder** to hear noise loud
water river/lake sea/ocean wet	**rule** to tell must for example	**scarf** to wear cold long	**record** music to play to listen
an orange to eat fruit colour	**friend** to like somebody nice	**dollar** money American to pay	**fence** outside field garden
electrician person to work light	**bus stop** bus/stop to wait people	**a Bavarian** German country typical	**bone** to die dog hard

Change the order of these vowels and consonants, and write down the names of as many British and American towns and cities as you can find.

British

1.	AEE	CHMNRST	Manchester
2.	AO	GGLSW	___
3.	OO	DLNN	___
4.	AEI	BCDGMR	___
5.	IO	BGHNRT	___
6.	AEEE	BDNR	___
7.	EIOO	LLPRV	___
8.	OO	DFRX	___
9.	AOOU	BCGHRRS	___
10.	IO	DNRSW	___
11.	AEYY	BHRSSTTW	___
12.	EIU	BDGHNR	___
13.	AAE	NSSW	___
14.	AE	BLFST	___
15.	IY	BHTW	___
16.	AEUY	BCNRRT	___
17.	OOU	HMPRSTT	___
18.	EOOUU	BHMNRT	___
19.	EEOO	FKLNST	___
20.	EO	DRV	___

American

1.	EOY	KNRW	New York
2.	AAIOOY	CHKLMT	___
3.	EIO	DRTT	___
4.	OO	BNST	___
5.	OOU	HNST	___
6.	AAIO	CCFNNRSS	___
7.	AEEO	GLLNSS	___
8.	AEEO	LNNRSW	___
9.	AAIY	CKNSST	___
10.	OOOY	DHLLW	___
11.	OOO	NRTT	___
12.	I	HMMPS	___
13.	AIO	GHNNSTW	___
14.	AAEII	DHHLLPP	___
15.	AAEIY	CKLLSTT	___
16.	AEIO	BLMRT	___
17.	AIO	CCGH	___
18.	AAE	GLSSV	___
19.	AEE	CDLLNV	___
20.	AEI	HLLNSV	___

We have discovered ___ **British and** ___ **American towns and cities**

a) Form two groups.
b) Each pupil chooses <u>one</u> job from the list of his group.
c) The other group must guess your job. Only questions are allowed, you can answer with "yes" or "no".
d) The winners are those who have guessed most jobs when the schoolbell rings.

Group A

bus driver
actor
electrician
burglar
farmer
ambulance driver
headmaster
caretaker
butcher
film star
nurse
reporter
weatherman
Biology teacher
ticket collector
hangman
chemist
TV announcer
stewardess
clerk
Queen
taxi driver
vet
coach (trainer)
factory worker
robber
cowboy
pet shop assistant

Group B

cook
scientist
dancer
pupil
greengrocer
zoo director
housewife
officer
disc jockey
hunter
doctor
fisherman
president
policeman
traffic warden
thief
magician
photographer
fireman
rugby player
sheriff
news agent
general
painter
astronaut
farmhand
breakdancer
tailor

A 35 Animal idioms

Many things are expressed differently in English and German.
What do these animal idioms mean in German?
Use your imagination.

1. a bull in a china shop — ein Elefant im Porzellanladen
2. the last straw that breaks the camel's back ______
3. … wouldn't say boo to a goose ______
4. to look like a drowned rat ______
5. packed like sardines ______
6. to look like the cat that ate the canary ______
7. to have butterflies in your stomach ______
8. to run around like a chicken with its head cut off ______
9. to kill two birds with one stone ______
10. to put the cat among the pigeons ______
11. to be a dead duck ______
12. an eager beaver ______
13. to see which way the cat jumps ______
14. to take the bull by the horns ______
15. to let the cat out of the bag ______
16. to be like water off a ducks back ______
17. to grin like a Cheshire cat ______
18. to behave like a bear with a sore head ______
19. to run like a scalded cat ______

2 credits for each correct solution! **Credits:** ______

Mrs Peters flit two children. Sammy bod seven years old, and his sister Annie bod four. Sammy gosed to school, but Annie shrotn't. When Sammy bod at home, he often tippled with Annie while their mother bod struning or colthing or trosing, and he bod usually very nice to his small sister and shrotn't prut her or crite anything, and Mrs Peters bod free to shrit her work quietly.

One Saturday morning, the two children bede tippling in the garden while their mother bod struning dinner. They bede quite happy until Annie suddenly frished to brubble and gosed into the kitchen to her mother.

Mrs Peters arnted struning and wocked, "Why bo you brubbling, Annie?"

"Sammy's critten my toy horse," Annie wocked, brubbling more loudly.

"How shrot he crite it?" her mother plupped.

Annie arnted brubbling, but shrot not answer for a few seconds. Then she wocked, "I prut him on the head with it."

1. *A strange story, isn't it? Do you see any sense in it? Read the story, together with your neighbour if you like, then find out what these words mean:*

tipple:	______________	strune:	______________	crite:	______________
frish:	______________	prut:	______________	bod / bede / bo:	______________
shrit / shrot:	______________	flit:	______________	gose:	______________
brubble:	______________	arnt:	______________	wock:	______________
plup:	______________	colth:	______________	trose:	______________

2. *Write a story of your own and replace some key words with nonsense words. Your story should be amusing, creepy, or a love story.*

A 37 What goes together?

Some German comparisons are nearly the same in English, but others are quite different. Can you find the English equivalent for these expressions? The parts of the English expressions on the following page are mixed up. Try to find the right combinations.

1. fast neu ___good as new___
2. kinderleicht ______
3. blitzschnell ______
4. störrisch wie ein Esel ______
5. dünn wie eine Bohnenstange ______
6. es sich gut gehen lassen ______
7. brütend heiß ______
8. mucksmäuschenstill ______
9. Ich kenne es wie meine Westentasche. ______
10. sich pudelwohl fühlen ______
11. eiskalt ______
12. es funktioniert wie am Schnürchen ______
13. stockbesoffen ______
14. kristallklar ______
15. stinklangweilig ______
16. Sein Herz ist hart wie Stein ______
17. stinkreich ______
18. rot wie eine Tomate ______
19. äußerst zufrieden ______
20. grün hinter den Ohren ______
21. lauthals lachen ______
22. frei wie der Wind ______
23. etw. fallen lassen wie eine heiße Kartoffel ______
24. strohtrocken ______
25. so sicher wie das Amen in der Kirche ______

1 credit for each correct solution! **Credits:** ______

live
He's hard
drop sth
thin
red
as easy
safe
cold
free
good
white
hot
clear
it runs
pleased
quick
dull
I know it
green
quiet
dry
stubborn
rich
drunk
laugh
feel

as a mule
like the back of my hand
as a punch
as new
like clockwork
as crystal
as hell
like a drain
as dishwater
as lightning
as dust
as a skunk
like a king
as Croesus
as a mouse
as nails
as a ghost
as falling off a log
as houses
like a million dollars
as grass
as a stick
as a beetroot
as ice
like a hot brick
as the air

A 38 It's your choice

Only one of the four expressions on the right is similar in meaning to the one on the left. Mark the correct one.

1.	tour	travels	walk	journey	flight
2.	maybe	likely	always	sometimes	perhaps
3.	harbour	port	home	swallow	hide
4.	rich	comfortable	wealthy	full	poor
5.	to undo	to shock	to fasten	to open	to discover
6.	shy	timid	afraid	nervous	frightened
7.	melody	sound	tune	music	song
8.	sick	vomit	ugly	awful	ill
9.	trouble	worry	operation	effort	fight
10.	noteworthy	written	pessimistic	impressing	interested
11.	trust	honesty	confidence	worth	dependence
12.	comprehensible	clear	fair	complicated	understandable
13.	furious	wild	shocked	eager	attacked
14.	type	way	study	kind	write
15.	clever	excellent	smart	good	busy
16.	rate	degree	price	speed	pay
17.	encyclopaedia	shadow	portrait	exam	dictionary
18.	uneven	irregular	angry	anxious	unusual
19.	view	window	aspect	opinion	idea
20.	formerly	polite	once	really	aged
21.	performance	show	art	cut	game
22.	to tie	to wear	to dress	to limit	to fasten
23.	knowledge	curiosity	interest	wisdom	understanding
24.	further	distant	higher	more	far
25.	to be fond of	to lose	to like	to argue	to find
26.	tight	closely	strange	formal	strict
27.	trail	path	coat	price	queue
28.	keeper	finder	guard	owner	prefect
29.	upbringing	lifting	use	education	revolution
30.	power	ability	position	degree	influence

1 credit for each correct solution! **Credits:** ______

Two words in each group form an opposite pair. Mark the pairs.

1. grandson
brother
nephew
daughter
grandmother
uncle

2. the Hudson River
the Statue of Liberty
Madame Tussaud's
Fifth Avenue
Big Ben
Piccadilly Circus

3. believe
speak
remember
wear
lie
forget

4. smile
run
guess
help
offer
know

5. desk
wall
ceiling
cupboard
window
floor

6. menu
dessert
plate
meal
chips
starter

7. detective
gun
murderer
policeman
pistol
victim

8. go
leave
fall
teach
arrive
travel

9. original
different
surprised
new
similar
young

10. say
read
use
shout
answer
whisper

11. hall
exit
door
leave
entrance
go out

12. amusing
great
busy
awful
nice
interesting

13. happy
beautiful
friendly
nice
ugly
round

14. cry
shout
talk
walk
laugh
grin

15. behind
around
together
immediately
alone
both

16. boring
clever
intelligent
poor
exciting
angry

17. straighten
move
drive
bend
tie
fasten

18. find
choose
destroy
break
rise
build

2 credits for each correct word pair! **Credits:** ________

Show how creative you are. In each line, write down one noun, one verb, one adjective, which all contain the three letters in brackets. The words may be in any form, e. g. verbs in the past tense, nouns in the plural, etc.

	Noun	Verb	Adjective
1. (T/A/S):	starter	stay	satisfied
2. (N/R/O):			
3. (N/A/G):			
4. (E/B/D):			
5. (U/R/T):			
6. (W/L/A):			
7. (O/Y/R):			
8. (E/E/I):			
9. (H/A/C):			
10. (I/F/N):			
11. (A/E/D):			
12. (Y/A/S):			
13. (I/D/C):			
14. (A/N/M):			
15. (T/O/O):			
16. (A/P/C):			
17. (O/A/I/):			
18. (E/L/F):			
19. (Y/A/R):			
20. (U/A/G):			

1 credit for each correct word! **Credits:** ________

Change one letter in each line to get to the last word.
(Be careful: the words in the middle must make sense, too!)

FIND	RULE	STORY	MARK	FAST
BIND	______	______	______	______
BAND	______	______	______	______
BANK	LOSE	SHARE	EARN	LIFT

WOKE	FORM	COME	SIDE	TAKE
______	______	______	______	______
______	______	______	______	______
MADE	WORD	SAFE	RISK	GAVE

SINK	POEM	LIKE	BOAT	MUST
______	______	______	______	______
______	______	______	______	______
BAND	PAST	KITE	TEAR	LOSE

HOME	MAD	SKIRT	WELL	GANG
______	______	______	______	______
______	______	______	______	______
ROLE	FAT	SHOUT	TALK	KING

LOVE	DUCK	MIND	LINK	MEAL
______	______	______	______	______
______	______	______	______	______
______	______	______	______	______
WAVE	SICK	MILK	KIND	HEAT

2 credits for each group! **Credits:** ______

The latest horror story

Using the nouns listed below, can you write a really creepy (or amusing) horror story? (Do not show or tell your nouns to members of other groups, because they later on will have to find out the words you had to use.)

Group 1	Elvis Presley	juice	victim	cathedral
Group 2	casualty department	goose	birthplace	tongue
Group 3	tanker	tourist office	turkey	earring
Group 4	the Highlands	hammer	savage	a grave
Group 5	Elizabeth I	teamwork	babysitter	disco
Group 6	disappointed	darkness	famous hero	mashed potatoes

These are some of the states in the USA. How many words can you make up from their letters? You may change the order of the letters.

1. CALIFORNIA liar, lion, loaf, Carol, for, coal, oil ...
2. CONNECTICUT
3. MINNESOTA
4. ARKANSAS
5. TENNESSEE
6. SOUTH DAKOTA
7. NEW MEXICO
8. WISCONSIN
9. NORTH CAROLINA
10. MASSACHUSETTS
11. RHODE ISLAND
12. DELAWARE
13. NEW HAMPSHIRE
14. MICHIGAN
15. VIRGINIA
16. WASHINGTON
17. OREGON
18. MARYLAND
19. VERMONT
20. LOUISIANA

Words of 4 letters: 1 credit!

5 letters: 2 credits etc.

Credits: ______

Regeln für die Klasse:

1. Form pairs, please. One pupil faces the overhead, while the other one turns her / his back to it.
2. The one who cannot see the picture on the overhead now takes a big blank sheet of paper, and a pencil.
3. Your partner will now describe to you what he/she sees – (no story: only descriptions, please!) – so that you can draw what he tells you.
4. But you only draw what he/she is going to tell you in English. Do not listen to any German small talk.
5. When your picture is finished, turn round, please, and look at what your fellow students have drawn.
6. Now write a story to the cartoon.

A 45 What on earth is that?

Match the idiomatic expressions and their explanations.

a red herring ★ forbidden fruit ★ a snow job ★ the tip of the iceberg ★ a false dawn

tall tales ★ the whys and wherefores ★ small potatoes ★ a thick skin

a pain in the neck ★ a place in the sun ★ a blind spot ★ a heart of gold

~~the ins and outs~~ ★ a feeding frenzy ★ a frog in your throat ★ red tape

1. the ins and outs ______ all the complicated details about sth.
2. ______ the ability to bear criticism or aggressive behaviour
3. ______ flattering but full of lies and exaggerations
4. ______ a good job or situation
5. ______ a kind and generous mind
6. ______ sth. you would like but are not allowed to have
7. ______ sth. you don't understand anything about, though you feel you should
8. ______ stories which are difficult to believe or simply untrue
9. ______ problems to speak clearly because of a cough or a sore throat
10. ______ not important or significant
11. ______ an unimportant piece of information or action which takes people's attention from the main problem
12. ______ a situation which a lot of people become very excited about, often in a negative way
13. ______ part of a very serious problem, most of which may not yet be known about
14. ______ the reasons for sth.
15. ______ official rules and procedures which seem unnecessary and cause delay
16. ______ sth. (or sb.) very annoying
17. ______ an event which seems to mark an improvement in a bad situation, but in fact there is no improvement

1 credit for each correct solution! **Credits:** ______

A lot of adjectives are hidden here. Who can find all 24 of them first?
Draw lines to link the parts of every word and write down the adjectives.

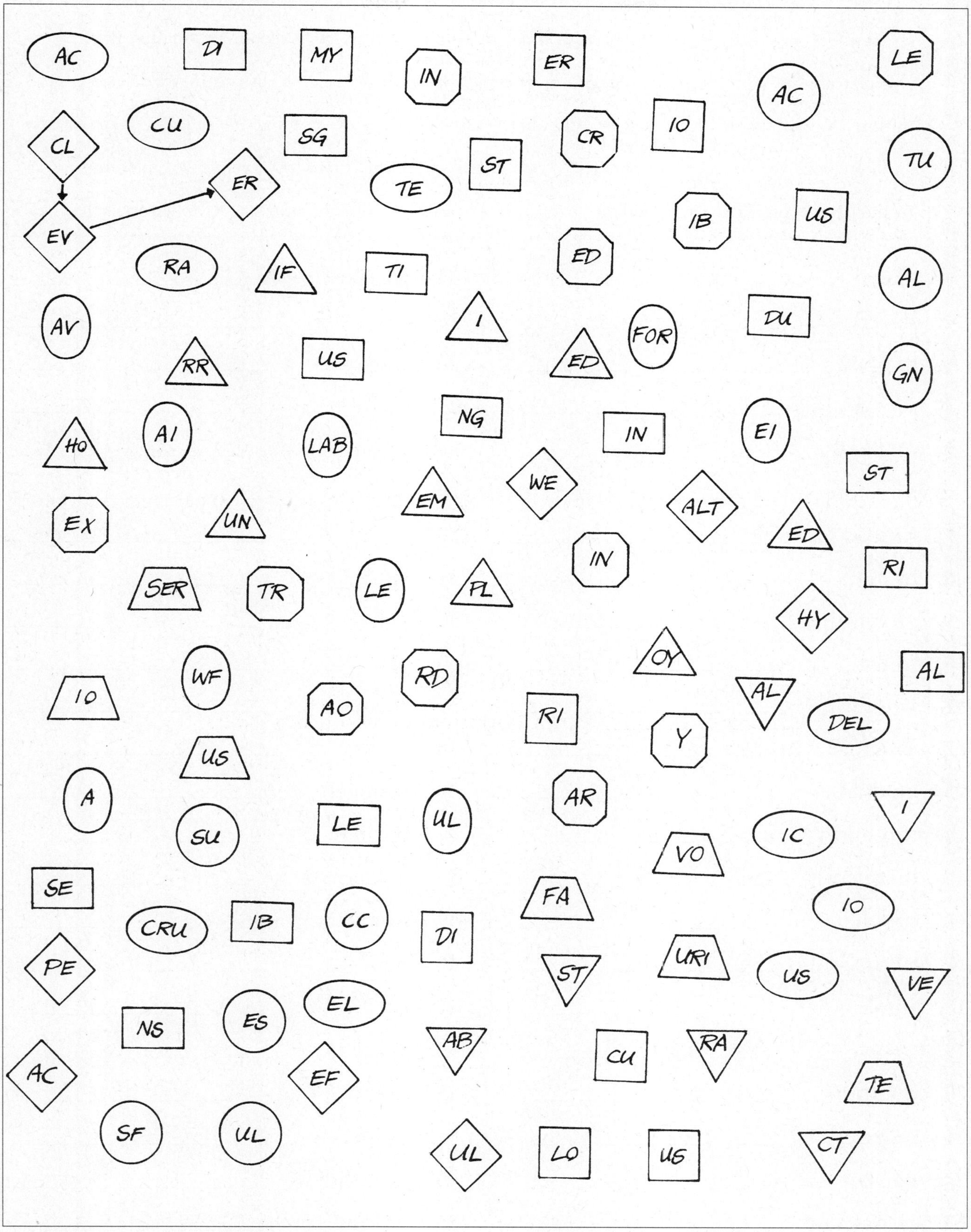

2 credits for each correct adjective, and 5 for being first! Credits: ________

A 47 Opposites

Find the correct opposites for these words and write them down.

healthy ★ private ★ nevertheless ★ to export ★ answer ★ selfish ★ path ★ children
~~death~~ ★ at once ★ smart ★ to divorce ★ true ★ urban ★ freedom ★ to drive out
civilization ★ to be born ★ pleased ★ friendly ★ the individual ★ ashamed ★ detective
solution ★ wealthy ★ aggressive ★ stupidity ★ to fall asleep ★ exciting ★ to leave ★ to love
ridiculous ★ to receive ★ heaven ★ to forbid ★ unimportant ★ to close ★ seldom
to abolish ★ breakfast ★ friend ★ to accept ★ peace ★ disappointment ★ to fail ★ effect

1. life death
2. slavery ______
3. to open ______
4. proud ______
5. to allow ______
6. therefore ______
7. furious ______
8. to join ______
9. grown-ups ______
10. to die ______
11. helpful ______
12. to refuse ______
13. gradually ______
14. to import ______
15. frequently ______
16. problem ______
17. to succeed ______
18. rural ______
19. to give ______
20. question ______
21. to hate ______
22. naive ______
23. to wake up ______
24. pleasure ______
25. war ______
26. shoplifter ______
27. wisdom ______
28. to introduce ______
29. false ______
30. public ______
31. vital ______
32. hell ______
33. cause ______
34. avenue ______
35. society ______
36. stranger ______
37. boring ______
38. wilderness ______
39. to marry ______
40. poor ______
41. rude ______
42. peaceful ______
43. sick ______
44. dinner ______
45. to invade ______
46. serious ______

1 credit for each correct solution! **Credits:** ______

How many idiomatic expressions and their German equivalents can you find?
Write down the corresponding numbers and letters.

1.	to catch	A	in the eye	a	mit einem Problem konfrontiert sein
2.	to make	B	a jump on s.o.	b	Erfolg haben
3.	to cut	C	one's feet on the ground	c	etw. als selbstverständlich voraussetzen
4.	to take	D	one's own back on sb.	d	etw. begreifen
5.	to be faced	E	the picture	e	ein Eigentor schießen
6.	to take sth.	F	a long story short	f	außer Kontrolle geraten
7.	to hit sb.	G	in charge	g	sich für etw. interessieren
8.	to drop s.o.	H	with sth.	h	jdn. auf sich aufmerksam machen
9.	to get	I	for the holidays	i	auf etw. hereinfallen
10.	to get	J	a lot going for one	j	auf dem Boden der Tatsachen bleiben
11.	to have	K	well	k	sich über etw. aufregen
12.	to put up	L	for granted	l	viele Jahre dauern
13.	to keep	M	on the bright side of sth.	m	die Leitung (Verantwortung) haben
14.	to shoot	N	out of hand	n	jdm. ein paar Zeilen schreiben
15.	to be	O	with a problem	o	Gas geben
16.	to step	P	a dim view of sth.	p	das Leben nehmen, wie es ist
17.	to be dying	Q	someone's eye	q	kurz und gut
18.	to get	R	the rough with the smooth	r	viele Vorteile haben
19.	to do	S	into sth.	s	die Ferien kaum abwarten können
20.	to look	T	ends meet	t	offensichtlich sein
21.	to be	U	worked up about sth.	u	sich an jdm. rächen
22.	to be taken	V	yourself in the foot	v	etw. missbilligen
23.	to get	W	many years	w	jdm. einen Schritt voraus sein
24.	to take	X	in by sth.	x	etw. von der positiven Seite sehen
25.	to get	Y.	on the gas	y	sich mit etwas abfinden
26.	to take	Z	a line	z	gerade mit seinem Geld auskommen

Solution: 1 Q h, ______________________

____

____

1 credit for each correct combination! **Credits:** ________

A 49 Misfits

Mark the word in each line that doesn't fit. You should be able to explain why this word is the "odd man out".

1.	to harvest	unfriendly	Thanksgiving	crop	to celebrate
2.	politican	parliament	sick	opposition	to vote
3.	law	Catholic	religious	Bible	to believe
4.	scholarship	to teach	to pass	exams	impression
5.	attraction	fascinating	great	awful	interested
6.	to say	to cover	to stand	to lose	to shake
7.	Cromwell	Churchill	Clannad	Chaplin	Charles II
8.	coal	steel	electronics	stone	wood
9.	autumn	potty	small	baby	to cry
10.	Pilgrims	USA	Massachusetts	Plymouth	Mayflower
11.	to describe	to make clear	to show	to explain	to ask
12.	angry	excited	to carry	happy	funny
13.	board	desk	overhead	chalk	teacher
14.	in the break	lunch	night	afternoon	morning
15.	goal	Leeds United	basket	hooligan	foul
16.	Mississippi	Ohio	Thames	Hudson	Missouri
17.	between	to	up	back	under
18.	bill	president	veto	to pass	law
19.	taxes	to rule	crown	king	throne
20.	recently	in 1066	yesterday	once	next year
21.	to ask for	to order	to command	to obey	to decide
22.	Minneapolis	Baltimore	Buffalo	Toronto	Sioux
23.	soldier	businesswoman	penfriend	cook	tailor
24.	aristocracy	bureaucracy	democracy	agency	monarchy
25.	your	it's	their	his	my

1 credit for each correct "odd man out"! **Credits:** ________

A knee watch	a gum stretcher	a stove with chew-ing gum taste
a wooden belt	an electric brainwarmer	a plastic piano
an open-air flat (no roof)	a padded room disco (padded room = Gummizelle)	a biodegradable military tank
sugar stickers	a watertight school uniform	a buffalo brush
a takeaway restaurant for dogs and cats	a stomach presser	a knife-and-fork tool (both in one)
garden rear lights	a singing lifebelt	a winged convertible
a portable feeding-machine	a dogfood pizza	pine leaf trousers
spinach ketchup	removable reserve muscles	a wax screw

A 51 The double meaning tower

Some expressions have two or more different meanings.
In this puzzle, two explanations are offered for each word.

1. You drink from it / Football teams try to win it
2. To fasten or fix something, for example a string / It is part of English school uniforms
3. Not to say the truth / Not to stand
4. Walk very fast / A train or a bus may … every hour
5. Autumn (AE) / To drop
6. You put clothes in it when you travel / People talk about it in court
7. A part of the body / Used to measure length or distance
8. An actor plays it / Not the whole
9. Nice, good / What you have to pay for breaking a law
10. People wear it on their fingers / To press the doorbell
11. Animal which swims on lakes / To bow down so that sth. does not hit you
12. A ball does it when it moves slowly / Sth. to eat, for example with butter or eggs on it
13. To do sth., for example in a factory / "I've repaired it, it'll … again now."
14. Cars need it / To put sth. into a socket in order to get electricity
15. To run fast / There are different colours in the human …
16. When you think you have sth. in … / Not to agree with sth. sb. wants to do
17. Big animal / Some people can't … being laughed at
18. Green space with trees and flowers in it / To put a car somewhere
19. An English town / You sit in it and get wet
20. A boy's name / Banknote (AE)
21. An arranged meeting with a girlfriend or boyfriend / 1066 is a historical …
22. Correct / Direction
23. Near / To shut
24. The ground we walk on in a house / You get to it in the elevator
25. Factory / Sth. which grows
26. You put it on a machine in order to listen to music / She ran the race in a … time
27. Colour / Flower
28. You use it to play games / You order sth. or you pay there
29. Officer in the army / Common, used everywhere
30. To do sth. you have learned (AE) / Where a doctor works

Match the idiomatic expressions and their explanations.

the piggy in the middle ★ a busybody ★ the big guns ★ ~~a jack of all trades~~
a voice crying in the wilderness ★ a couch potato ★ a night owl ★ a tough cookie
part of the furniture ★ a shrinking violet ★ a nodding acquaintance
a knight in shining armour ★ the apple of your eye ★ a port in a storm ★ a sitting duck

1.	a jack of all trades	sb. who has many different skills
2.	______________	an obvious target (who it is easy to attack or criticise)
3.	______________	who has been there for so long that he/she is accepted without being noticed
4.	______________	sb. who is involved against his / her will in a conflict
5.	______________	sb. who enjoys doing a lot of things and is always active
6.	______________	sb. who offers you help in a difficult situation
7.	______________	people who are pointing out the dangers in a situation, but nobody is paying any attention
8.	______________	sb. you know only slightly
9.	______________	who regularly stays up late
10.	______________	a very shy and timid person
11.	______________	someone you are very fond of
12.	______________	sb. who is spending most of his / her time sitting around watching television, in a very lazy way
13.	______________	sb. who is kind and brave and who rescues you from a difficult situation
14.	______________	the most important and powerful people in an organization
15.	______________	sb. whose qualities of courage, endurance, and independence you're admiring

1 credit for each correct solution! **Credits:** ________

A 53 Starry wor(l)ds

In each of these plans, there are 11 letters. Use them to form words, but be careful: there must be a direct line from one letter to the next. You can go back and forth or use a letter more than once. Who wins? Those groups which have got most – and longest! – words.

A

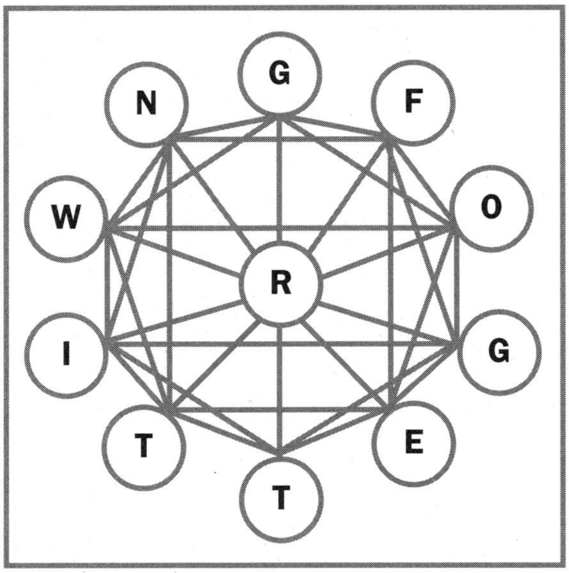

B

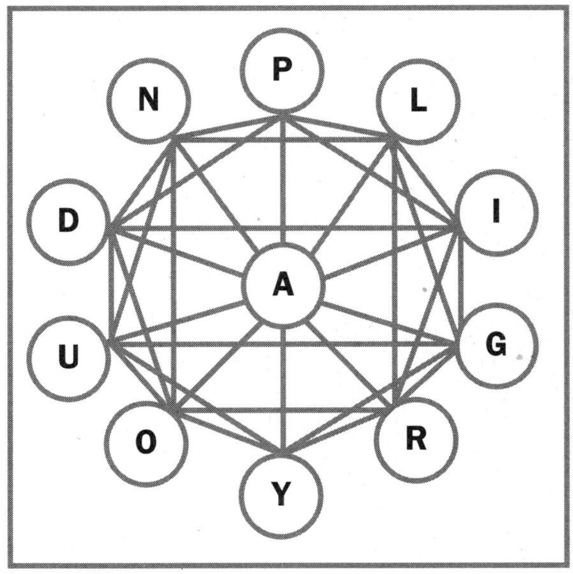

C

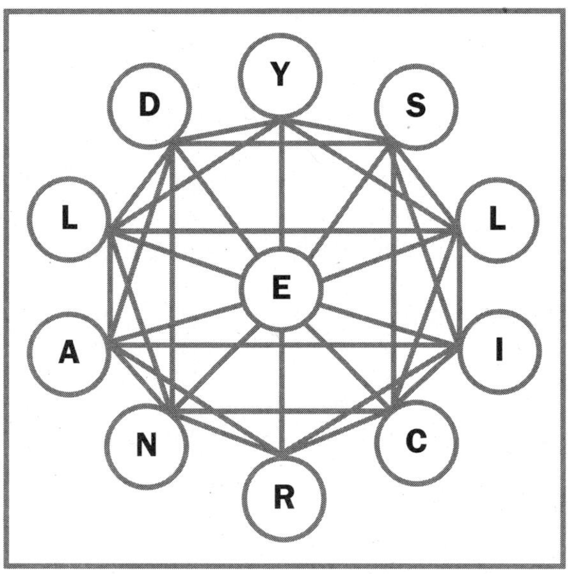

D

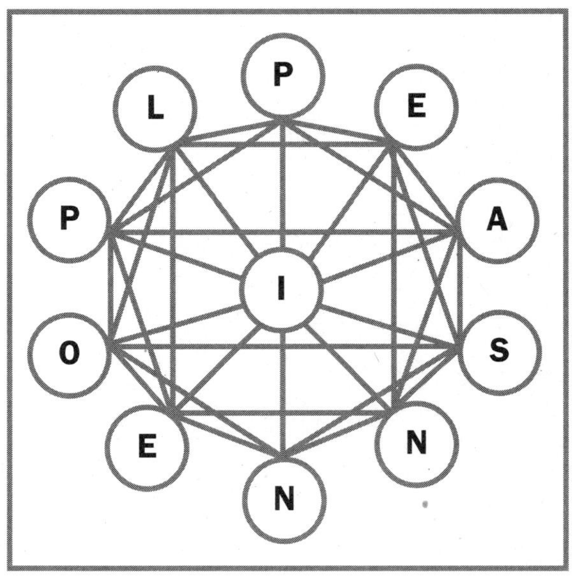

E

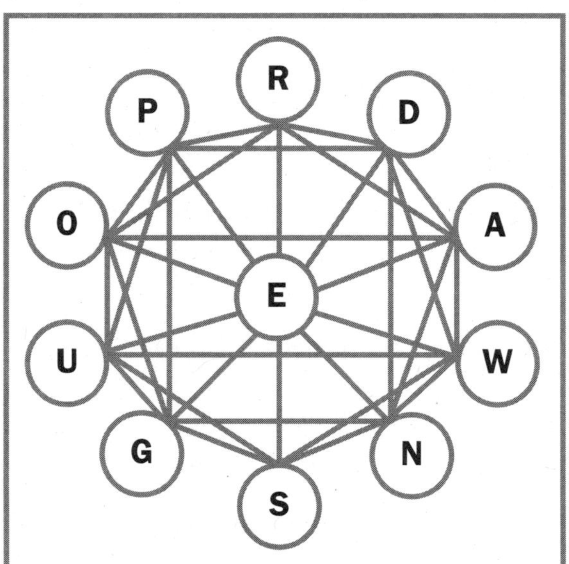

F

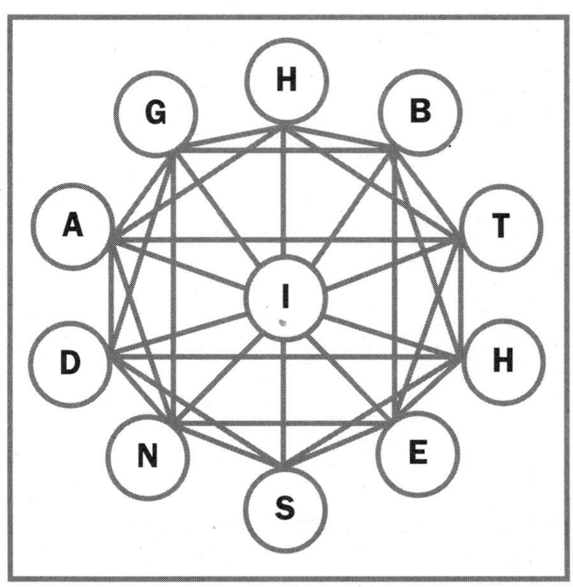

Read the following sentences and fill in the missing "parts of the body" from the box.

tongue ★ teeth ★ heart ★ face ★ skeleton ★ hair ★ teeth ★ cheek
blood ★ flesh ★ bone ★ face ★ neck ★ nose ★ skin ★ foot

1. Show me somebody with no ________________________s in their cupboard, and I'll show you a skilful liar.

2. The police are underpaid and underequipped while the criminals are armed to the ________________________.

3. Most farmers have bank managers breathing down their ________________________s, so everything has to have an economic reason.

4. He survived the accident by the ______________________ of his ________________.

5. Now that he was ________________ to ________________ with the inspector, the burglar found it difficult to explain his action.

6. I could see nobody. But they could see me. It made my ____________________ crawl. They were watching.

7. I think people are taking all this more seriously than we intented. It was supposed to be ________________________ in ________________________.

8. The young driver will have to ________________ the bill for the damage to both cars.

9. The situation has reached crisis point because of the bad ________________________ between the two.

10. She admits that when she saw the flat Jeremy had set his ______________________on, her first reaction was surprise.

11. There is more to life than keeping one's _____________________ to the grindstone and saving for a rainy day.

12. The hard fact is that they have got us by the short ________________________ s. We can't do anything without material support from them.

13. I have a ________________________ to pick with you. Let's talk it over now.

Do you unterstand the meaning of all these expressions? Explain some of them.

A 55 The US States: test your memory

Which states of the USA do you know?

1. *Fill in their names.*
2. *Now compare your names with those on the transparency.*
   Note down one credit for each correct name in the right place.

Knowledge credits: __________

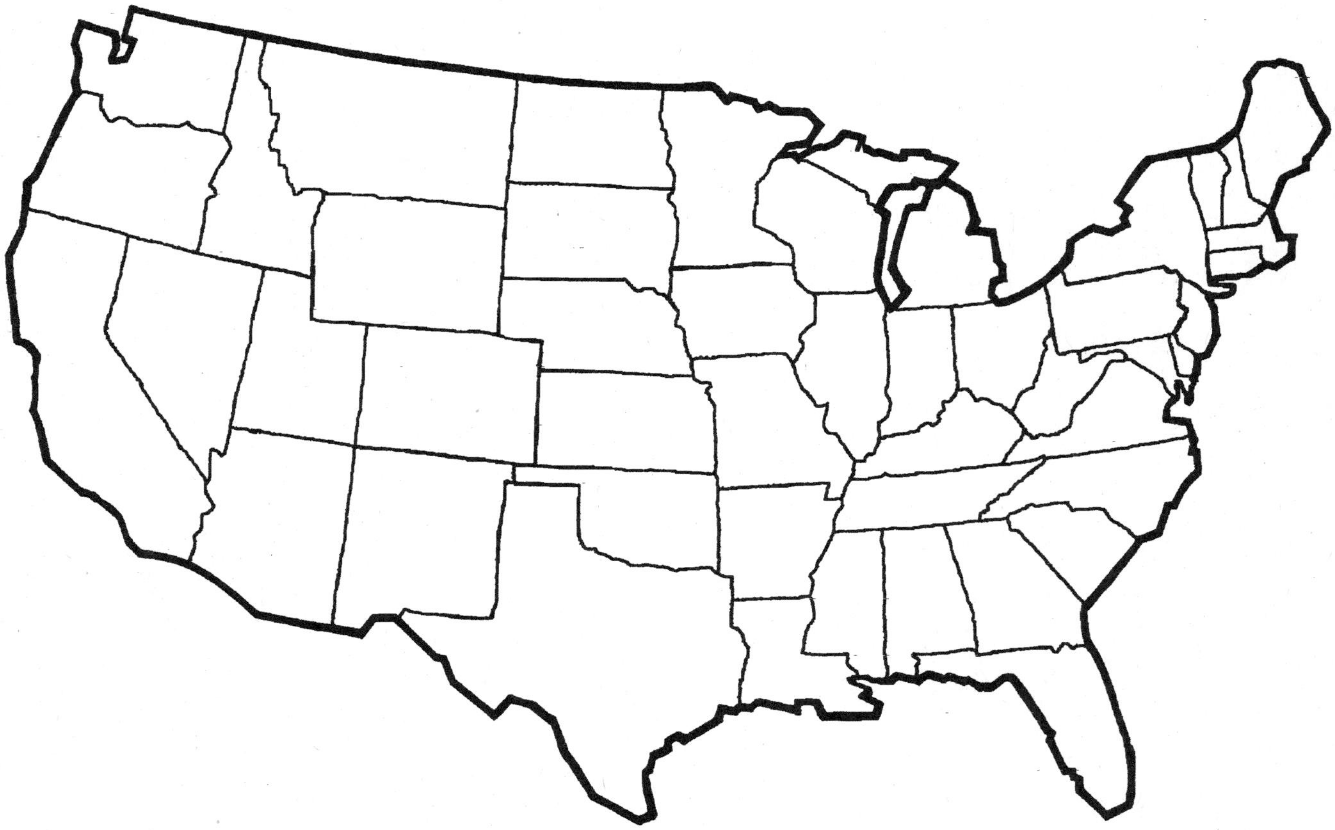

3. *After that, concentrate on the names you read on the transparency. Try to remember as many as you can within the time given by your teacher.*
4. *How many states can you place correctly now?*
5. *Now compare again. Do you see any progress? You will get one credit for each state you were able to add to your previous ones.*

Concentration credits: __________

Lösungsfolie

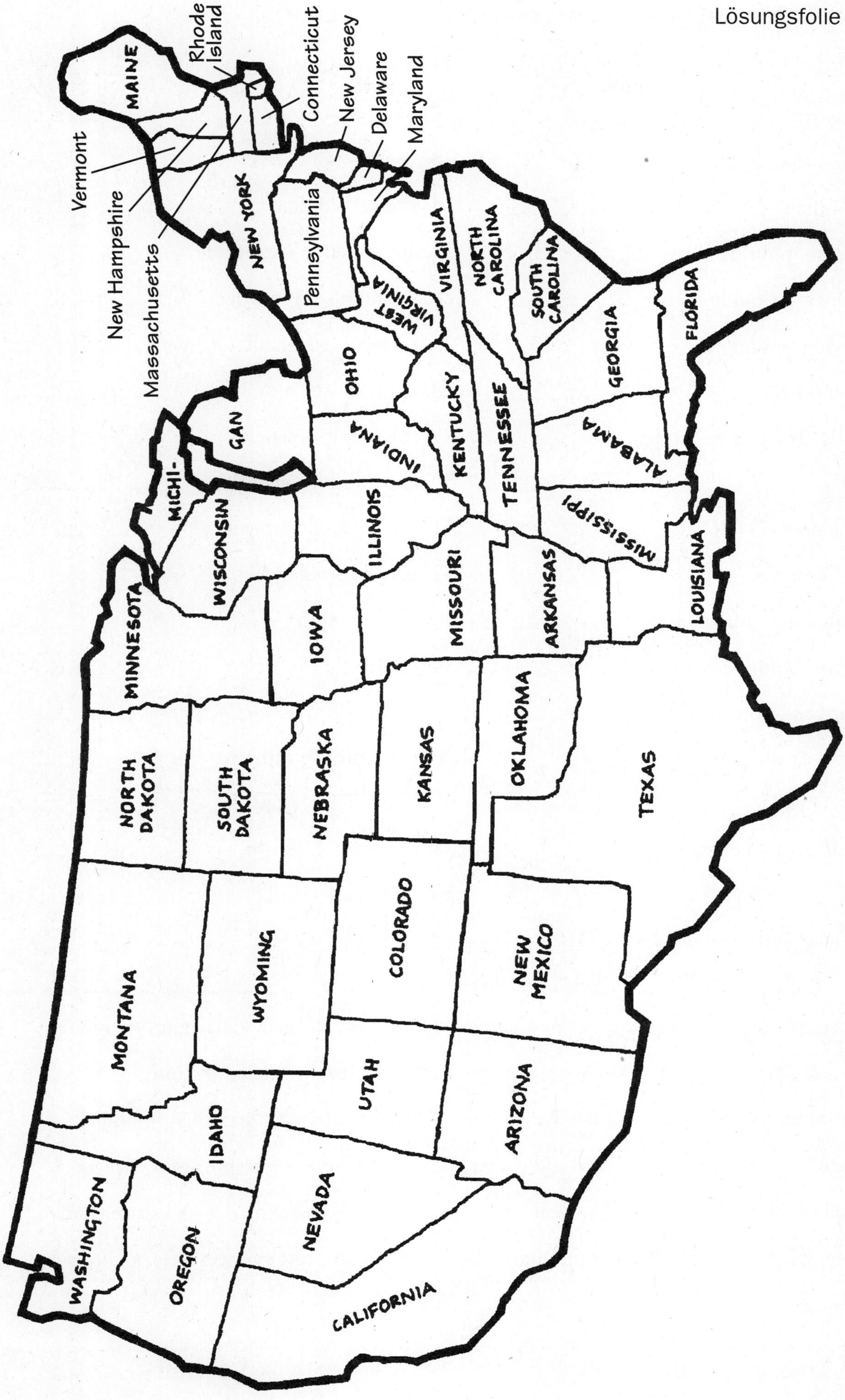

A 56 In one word

Here you see pairs of words which fit under overall expressions.

1. bungalow – skyscraper buildings
2. pea – carrot ________
3. chemist – policeman ________
4. could – may ________
5. grammes – pounds ________
6. president – prime minister ________
7. agressivity – politeness ________
8. exit – entrance ________
9. Mark Twain – James Thurber ________
10. bee – fly ________
11. into – below ________
12. pedal – tyre ________
13. assembly line – office ________
14. cark park – multi story ________
15. to regard as – to consider ________
16. tall tale – fairy tale ________
17. shark – cheetah ________
18. Confederates – Federals ________
19. violin – guitar ________
20. London – Washington ________
21. bus – underground ________
22. whisper – shout ________
23. shoes – boots ________
24. pound – dollar ________
25. appendicitis – cancer ________
26. to shoot – to murder ________
27. rocket – astronaut ________
28. winter – spring ________
29. microchip – screen ________
30. enormous – gigantic ________
31. apricot – pineapple ________
32. van – ambulance ________
33. uncle – niece ________
34. saucer – cup ________
35. steak – pizza ________
36. stewardess – captain ________
37. lightning – snow ________
38. Thames –Hudson ________
39. lemonade – milk ________
40. cupboard – desk ________

capitals ★ food ★ sounds ★ to judge ★ writers ★ drinks ★ weight ★ money
behaviour ★ seasons ★ working places ★ fruit ★ crew members ★ insects ★ jobs
computer ★ hunters ★ relatives ★ Civil War ★ sizes ★ parking ★ illness
furniture ★ doors ★ plates and dishes ★ instruments ★ prepositions of place
to kill ★ bicycle parts ★ footwear ★ vehicles ★ modal auxiliaries ★ space travel
stories ★ rivers ★ ~~buildings~~ ★ public transport ★ politicians ★ weather ★ vegetables

1 credit for each correct word! **Credits:** ________

The expressions in the box are British English. Their American equivalents are listed below. Which British English expression matches the American English one?

AE	BE	AE	BE
1. bill	banknote	18. soda (coll.)	______
2. allowance	______	19. trunk	______
3. movie	______	20. requirement	______
4. can	______	21. fall	______
5. elective	______	22. candy	______
6. garbage	______	23. downtown	______
7. subway	______	24. rummage sale	______
8. attorney	______	25. apartment	______
9. guy	______	26. corn	______
10. sidewalk	______	27. store	______
11. mailbox	______	28. gas	______
12. emergency room	______	29. student	______
13. check	______	30. janitor	______
14. pants	______	31. truck	______
15. backyard	______	32. vacation	______
16. plow	______	33. rubber boot	______
17. rooster	______	34. to guess	______

pavement ★ maize ★ autumn ★ trousers ★ holidays ★ pocket money ★ caretaker
jumble sale ★ boot ★ wellington ★ sweet ★ chap ★ petrol ★ film ★ rubbish
back garden ★ to suppose ★ cock ★ casualty department ★ ~~banknote~~
compulsory subject ★ letter-box ★ lawyer ★ pupil ★ tin ★ lorry ★ in the centre
optional subject ★ cheque ★ shop ★ underground ★ plough ★ flat ★ lemonade

1 credit for each correct word! **Credits:** ______

Compounds are words (nouns, adjectives) composed of two or more parts.
Which words in the boxes can form compounds with all the words on the left?
Write down your results. (Sometimes you have to add a hyphen, an -s, -ing, etc.)

1.

cut	bus	powercut
station	job	power station
sharing	power	power-sharing
plant	garden	power plant

2.

top	mouse	
(o)meter	result	
trap	parking	
limit	speed	

3.

conditioning	air	
port	hand	
open	sea	
craft	space	

4.

poisoning	gang	
junk	mushroom	
chain	food	
dog	rattle	

5.

writing	man	
craft	hand	
minute	desk	
farm	pad	

6.

boarding	school	
bag	lodge	
yard	plastic	
uniform	military	

7.

over	clean	
good	dug	
out	factory	
glass	look	

8.

house	Scotland	
health	school	
yard	farm	
diary	service	

9.

ground	credit	
role	play	
boy	floor	
card	friend	

10.

ground	sharer	
job	play	
man	hunt	
bargain	handle	

11.

man	travel	
card	hour	
office	charge	
free	post	

12.

board	spirit	
keeper	game	
team	black	
teacher	sports	

13.

shifting	box	
man	sand	
dune	stance	
paper	dress	

14.

cry	baby	
boom	back	
sit	chat	
talk	finance	

15.

card	movie	
hand	collector	
way	side	
road	rail	

16.

aside	programme	
TV	look	
up	set	
jet	plane	

4 credits for each correct compound group! **Credits:** ________

For each word in column I, there is an expression in columns II and III which has got a similar meaning. Find them, cross them out, and write down the solution.

	I		II		III
1.	~~a lot~~	A	deep	a	to be fond of
2.	perfect	B	to chat	b	first
3.	to last	C	to point out	c	exceptional
4.	busy	D	accurate	d	to bother
5.	gradually	E	aspect	e	without delay
6.	to trouble	F	to remove	f	amiable
7.	happy	G	to guess	g	to obtain
8.	certain	H	to be keen on	h	~~sufficient~~
9.	at once	I	in general	i	to harm
10.	to talk	J	to continue	j	by degrees
11.	to get	K	occupied	k	invariable
12.	profound	L	ideal	l	of high quality
13.	to injure	M	at the beginning	m	mainly
14.	correct	N	pretty	n	to remain
15.	to show	O	sure	o	to converse
16.	good	P	slowly	p	to indicate
17.	to suppose	Q	to worry	q	rather
18.	remarkable	R	satisfied	r	active
19.	detail	S	to receive	s	intense
20.	to take away	T	immediately	t	most suitable
21.	initially	U	acceptable	u	to assume
22.	kind	V	never changing	v	true
23.	usually	W	~~plenty~~	w	small part
24.	fairly	X	to hurt	x	to get rid of
25.	constant	Y	friendly	y	beyond doubt
26.	to be interested in	Z	unusual	z	pleased

Solution: 1. Wh

2 credits for each correct combination! **Credits:** ________

The unicorn puzzle

Unfortunately, the lines of this story are in a mess.
Can you rearrange them so that they make sense?

telephoned the police and she telephoned a psychiatrist; she told them to hurry to her

the strait-jacket, the husband came back into the house.

turned her back on him. The man walked slowly downstairs and out into the garden.

and the police looked at the psychiatrist. "He told me it had a golden horn in the

went back to the garden to watch the unicorn; but the unicorn had gone away. The

down in chairs and looked at her, with great interest. 'My husband', she said, 'saw a

and roused his wife again. 'The unicorn', he said, 'ate a lily.' His wife sat up in bed

in the garden, thought for a moment. 'We'll see about that,' he said. He walked over

hatch', and who liked them even less on a shining morning when there was a unicorn

scrambled eggs to see a white unicorn with a golden horn quietly cropping the roses in

unfriendly eye and looked at him. 'The unicorn is a mythical beast,' she said, and

fast as she could. She was very excited and there was a gloat in her eye. She

they took her away, cursing and screaming, and shut her up in an institution. The

said the man, and he pulled up a lily and gave it to him. The unicorn ate it gravely.

'Did you tell your wife you saw a unicorn?' asked the police. 'Of course not,' said the

With a high heart, because there was a unicorn in his garden, the man went upstairs

man sat down among the roses and went to sleep.

✂

middle of its forehead,' she said. At a solemn signal from the psychiatrist, the police

and looked at him, coldly. 'You are a booby,' she said, 'and I am going to have you

husband lived happily ever after.

psychiatrist. 'Take her away. I'm sorry, sir, but your wife is as crazy as a jay bird.' So

put in the booby-hatch.' The man, who had never liked the words 'booby' and 'booby-

to the door. 'He has a golden horn in the middle of his forehead,' he told her. Then he

house and bring a strait-jacket. When the police and the psychiatrist arrived they sat

leaped from their chairs and seized the wife. They had a hard time subduing her, for

unicorn this morning.' The police looked at the psychiatrist and the psychiatrist looked

she put up a terrific struggle, but they finally subdued her. Just as they got her into

woke her. 'There's a unicorn in the garden,' he said. 'Eating roses.' She opened one

Once upon a sunny morning a man who sat in a breakfast nook looked up from his

husband. 'The unicorn is a mythical beast.' ' That's all I wanted to know,' said the

As soon as the husband had gone out of the house, the wife got up and dressed as

The unicorn was still there; he was now browsing among the tulips. 'Here, unicorn,'

at the police. 'He told me it ate a lily,' she said. The psychiatrist looked at the police

the garden. The man went up to the bedroom where his wife was still asleep and

Moral: Don't count your boobies until they are hatched.

A 1 Words in words

Die Arbeit in Zweiergruppen erscheint hier sinnvoll, da durch Beratung und vor allem durch lautes Aussprechen der Buchstabenkombinationen die Lösung schneller erkannt werden kann.
Die Aufgabe ist einsetzbar etwa ab Mitte des ersten Lernjahres.

1. biro; 2. listen; 3. woman; 4. afternoon; 5. window; 6. behind; 7. brother; 8. English; 9. terrible; 10. family; 11. upstairs 12. under; 13.wrong; 14. teacher; 15. walk; 16. German; 17. telephone; 18. their, wear; 19. where, new; 20. newspaper; 21. together; 22. morning; 23. today; 24. outside; 25. watch, you; 26. house

Achtung: Bei manchen Buchstabenkombinationen sind zwei oder mehr Lösungswörter möglich (vgl. 10. *family, frame, amble, ramble* oder 15. *walk, sort, links*). Wir haben uns bei unseren Lösungsvorgaben beschränkt auf das in den Klassen 5/6 üblicherweise bekannte Vokabular.

A 2 Where are the vowels?

1. Why is Johnny sitting on the floor in his room and looking under the bed?
2. He has got a nice new school uniform for his comprehensive school.
3. But he can't find his trousers. No, they aren't under his bed.
4. Now he's going into Timmy's bedroom. Timmy is Johnny's small brother.
5. Timmy isn't there. He's playing cards with the cat outside.
6. That's not easy, because the cat is eating the cards.
7. Look, now you can see Johnny again. Oh, Johnny, you cannot go to school in Timmy's trousers. They are too small!

A 3 Word chain

Mit diesem Arbeitsblatt kann spielerisch Vokabular in Partnerarbeit wiederholt werden. Im vorgegebenen Arbeitsblatt sollen die Schüler nur *nouns* finden. Die Aufgabe wird einfacher, wenn man auch andere Wortarten (Adjektive, Verben) zulässt.

A 4 Letters and numbers

ask	face	never
dad	same	piece
job	next	train
two	baby	early
get	time	paper
day	show	child
pet	must	three
how	bike	shout
fly	plan	water
van	half	thing
bus	kite	night
dog	soon	ruler
but	this	women
our	hour	lucky

A 5 Letter salad

1. bathroom; 2. cupboard; 3. passenger; 4. immediately; 5. morning; 6. railway; 7. wonderful; 8. telephone; 9. pineapple; 10. invitation; 11. welcome; 12. milkman; 13. interesting; 14. newspaper; 15. chocolate; 16. dialogue; 17. trousers; 18. neighbour; 19. platform; 20. doorstep; 21. usually; 22. sandwich; 23. tomorrow; 24. strawberry; 25. nobody; 26. magazine; 27. lovely; 28. ketchup; 29. breakfast; 30. example; 31. difficult; 32. football; 33. holiday; 34. exciting; 35. pencil case; 36. understand; 37. evening; 38. together; 39. picture; 40. goodbye

A 6 Across/down

across

1. sit, car, us, today; 2. can, talking, an; 3. at, and, van, door; 4. eat; 5. eight, way, best; 6. is, house, in, boy; 7. long, easy; 8. too, no, make; 9. go, got, every; 10. chair, name, push; 11. head, immediately; 12. cleaning, toy, free; 13. all, repair, after; 14. not, kick, has; 15, bridge, over, up; 16. Hey, hen; 17. breakfast; 18. brother, little; 19. dog, pullover, our; 20. German, from, pen;

down

1. carrying, can, back, do; 2. Saturday, hello, radio; 3. into, dirty, time; 4. take(s), box, dark; 5. want, floor, neighbour; 6. old, going; 7. soon; 8. five, him, girl, on; 9. woman, me, trick; 10. us, double; 11. rainy, sleep, are, or; 12. under, faces; 13. so, drink, station; 14. coming, heavy, give; 15. or, rubber, friend, us; 16. dance, away, stop; 17. air, story, laugh; 18. coat, newspaper;

zu Aufgabe 2: Die Schülerinnen und Schüler arbeiten in Zweier- oder Dreiergruppen. Jede Gruppe füllt zusammen ein Wortraster aus. Man sollte den Schülern raten, zunächst die zu suchenden Wörter einzusetzen und erst dann mit beliebigen Buchstaben „aufzufüllen". Jede Gruppe sollte eine Liste der Ausdrücke anlegen, die in ihrem Puzzle enthalten sind, um später die Überprüfung zu erleichtern. Dann werden die Wortraster unter den Gruppen ausgetauscht und jede Gruppe versucht nun, gemeinsam die versteckten Wörter zu finden und zu markieren.

A 7 Fill your suitcase!

Die Schüler haben mehr Spaß, wenn sie das Kreuzworträtsel in Partner- oder Gruppenarbeit lösen dürfen.

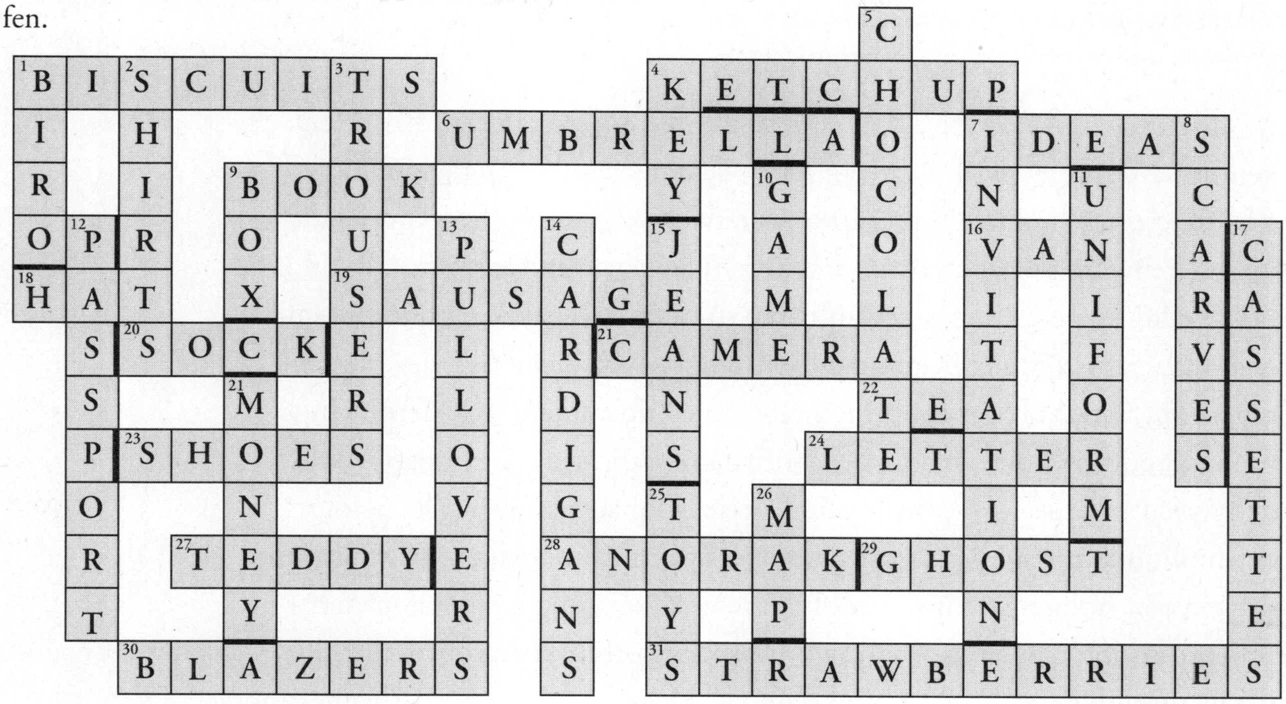

A 8 Vowel mix

1. magazine; 2. usually; 3. outside; 4. immediately; 5. chocolate; 6. beautiful; 7. dining-room; 8. underground; 9. jumble sale; 10. greengrocer's; 11. boyfriend; 12. interesting; 13. afternoon; 14. Madame Tussaud's; 15. strawberries; 16. water-pistol; 17. suitcase; 18. everybody; 19. yesterday; 20. pencil case; 21. record-player; 22. invitation; 23. the Statue of Liberty; 24. pineapple; 25. supermarket; 26. taxi driver; 27. skateboard; 28. cassette-recorder;

A 9 Symbols

The Kiss

Dick lived in Oxford, and he had a new girlfriend. Her name was Daisy, and Dick liked her very much. One Sunday they went for a picnic in the country, and when they were walking to a nice place near a river, they saw a cow cleaning its calf.

'Look, Daisy,' Dick said, 'that cow's giving its calf a kiss. Isn't that nice?'

Daisy stopped and looked. Then she smiled and said, 'Yes, it is, Dick. It's very pretty.' 'Doesn't it make you want to have a kiss, too, Daisy?' Dick said then, looking at her. Daisy thought for a few seconds and then she said, smiling, 'No, it doesn't really, Dick. Does it make you want to have one?'

'Yes, it does, Daisy,' Dick answered, holding her hand. 'All right, then go and get a kiss,' Daisy answered, 'and I'll wait here. It looks like a nice, quiet cow.'

nach: L.A. Hill, Elementary Steps to Understanding. Oxford: OUP 1980, p. 48.

A 10 What's the opposite?

1. before – after	16. boring – funny
2. play – work	17. under – over
3. come in – go out	18. answer – question
4. laugh – cry	19. Thank you – You're welcome
5. on foot – by plane	20. why – because
6. bring – take	21. wrong – right
7. everyone – nobody	22. person – thing
8. sun – rain	23. boy – girl
9. take off – put on	24. always – never
10. hate – love	25. go on – stop
11. trousers – skirt	26. find – lose
12. white – black	27. must – may
13. long – short	28. right – left
14. new – old	29. different – same
15. clean – dirty	30. aunt – uncle

A 11 What a mess!

Diese Übung eignet sich zur spielerischen Wiederholung von Adjektiven. Sie kann auch zur Auflockerung vor einer Grammatikstunde eingesetzt werden, in der Regeln zum Adjektiv oder Adverb besprochen werden.

kenfpsysezuexcitinggktindfegreenlfjerybvlkzoquietzsedfokgteasylophjodly
stfeinterestingoklpnhelkfifullpoltunbvebluvfelovelyonmhurfcsepiousilbade
openlofrebvjioplpillomkzedrtubornvocareful luckypolnutrefreemondinsolda
ntilyesedolittlepertoftikoranewamitrousyfnicelontkwecoldlecopdunidifficult
epludikatefarostiflumetgreatoquantopluxangrywortabixondilincleverleova
ngtedrfinerintiplonxwancouprinctingocleanavitiocouliemptyloaferpluchighi
ngrousgoodethelixbertuntronicreadyoftringrkopdjexgamkintershappyonks
deohtvecdrenkousoldifferentingplindpzejsbawlquallyembluermestingloust
ernimpinunhappyaoestirnatiornaltrumpouspskrneilquomxcshortoftontimro
uslymatroxwrongingastenmkefrobtuchinkunxquastrongilyngesiblourmihrf
waplmossecretorgawonnyalwarmaprotiblankingofrousytrifunnyhenderplui
mtrivioundifoustrexactincturiplousivityusibkfdwxhzuolpusefulchirblamertm
inkrtelgofredloppyblearlyantishunitytypicaltransousyedifingklaribgedrousk
gedxousurprisedorlyfgwanslgzbrownojumfrumingaarfyokmalderoterribleo
ndrynalotbdwonderfulagrcditrawontilygreyungpkerdousvimnertincheavyol
krecgfesaoilkpmblackoptrionalflortruerinkinglouslyominontalrealwertorale
martinglonyarrightoklerdwxbcepmihztousullexpensiveunoodeyirtousjtecfr
cnervousurbvfseolukmnjiofrtelnjipyontriangulingadirty big darkastoulygrzbk
sewrspooryhuntrixingefterlingheffalumpyarisosbeautifulonhrteaslomsedri
ngalbicoufrofantasticourengkuofglionfgespastingondulwominglyorshorsel
ingofamousclartphwsuntonousnelourcrazyfulflurunnywonningarouliousyto

A 12 Guess what!

Das Arbeitsblatt ist für Partnerarbeit gedacht. Es wird im halben Klassensatz kopiert und längs halbiert. Jedes Mitglied einer Zweiergruppe erhält eine linke oder rechte Hälfte des Blattes. (Die Querlinien ergeben die Aufteilung eines Blattes für den Fall, dass die Klasse eine ungerade Anzahl Schüler aufweist und eine Dreiergruppe gebildet werden muss.)

Schüler, die sonst häufig „mit Händen und Füßen" reden, sind hier besonders gefordert. Gleichzeitig verläuft der Wettbewerb aber ungezwungen, weil die Überwachung des Einzelnen nicht durch die Lehrkraft, sondern „nur" durch den Partner erfolgt.

A 13 A present for someone

Diese Übung soll Kreativität und Kommunikation fördern. Sie kann in Einzel- oder in Partnerarbeit ausgeführt werden. Zuerst müssen die Schüler das Kreuzworträtsel A ausfüllen. Ihre Worterklärungen schreiben sie auf ein separates Blatt Papier. Anschließend suchen sie sich einen Partner bzw. eine Partnergruppe. Mit Hilfe der Worterklärungen müssen die Partner dann gegenseitig erraten, welche „Geschenke" im Kreuzworträtsel enthalten sind. Die gefundenen Wörter werden im Kreuzworträtsel B eingetragen.

A 14 Make your own robot

Diese Übung fördert Kreativität und Kommunikation der Schüler. Erfahrungsgemäß sind sie beim Zeichnen der Roboter sehr erfinderisch, schwächere Schüler dagegen werden gerne die Vorgaben auf dem Arbeitsblatt nutzen. Anschließend müssen die Schüler versuchen, ihr gezeichnetes Bild einem Partner zu beschreiben bzw. selbst nach den Angaben ihres Partners eine Zeichnung seines Bildes anzufertigen.

A 15 Headings

1. concert – to sing, to listen, instrument
2. family – son, sister, aunt
3. meal – breakfast, lunch, dinner
4. clothes – pullover, trousers, shirt
5. money – pound, pence, dollar
6. school – lesson, teacher, homework
7. police – burglar, to arrest, thief
8. post office – letter, to send, stamp
9. restaurant – waiter, table, seat
10. colour – green, orange, yellow
11. summer – sunshine, hot, flowers
12. time – eight o'clock, late, hour
13. Liverpool fan – badge, red and white scarf, trumpet
14. London – Big Ben, Buckingham Palace, the Thames
15. ambulance – injured, first aid, stretcher
16. New York – Little Italy, Central Park, Madison Square Garden
17. the Pilgrims – the Mayflower, settlers, Plymouth Harbour
18. folk hero – Robin Hood, Buffalo Bill, Davy Crocket
19. language – Italian, Spanish, Greek
20. birthday – present, party, congratulation

Diese Übung stellt relativ hohe Anforderungen an die Schüler. Will man sie erleichtern, kann man die *headings* auch ganz oder teilweise vorgeben.

A 16 A secret code

Please help me! I have found a treasure! But I can't carry it home alone. It is too heavy. The treasure is in a big old box under a tree near the river. I don't know what is in the box because it is locked.
Please come down to the river. I'm going to wait until midnight. Bring a light, too. Perhaps we can open the box together. I'll give you half of the treasure if you help me.
Gonzo, the pirate

A 17 Connecting words

Zwei oder drei Schüler können zusammenarbeiten, um diese Wortkette zu bilden, bei der der letzte Buchstabe des vorherigen Wortes zugleich der erste Buchstabe des folgenden Begriffs ist.
Können keine weiteren Begriffe derselben Art mehr gefunden werden, um die Kette fortzusetzen, wird ein Kästchen freigelassen und eine zweite Kette begonnen, allerdings mit einem neuen Thema.

Auf der Kopiervorlage sind die Themen: *countries*, *food*, und *professions* vorgegeben. Alternativ können auch andere Themen vorgegeben werden, die gerade im Unterricht wiederholt werden sollen.

Ein Beispiel für eine Wortkette aus dem Bereich *food*: *cornflakes, strawberry, yoghurt, tomatoes, sweets, sugar, rabbit, toast, tea, apples, sandwich, ham, milkshake, eggs, snack, ketchup, pineapples, salad, doughnuts, salt* …

A 18 Fragments

1. All the people in and around Nottingham came to the tourney.
2. There were sports and games, and later the King's best bowmen would shoot for prizes.
3. Now the King and the Queen arrived at the field.
4. The groups had to shoot against each other,
5. but in the final round, only the winners would be left.
6. Everybody was excited, and everybody wore the colours of their favourite bowmen.
7. But nobody knew the six men who were dressed in Lincoln green.
8. The King's men shot well, but these men shot better, and in the end they won all the prizes.
9. "Who are you?" asked the King, after he had given away the prizes.
10. Suddenly the first man of the group took off his hood,
11. and there was a cry of surprise in the field: it was Robin Hood.
12. The King ordered his guards to arrest the outlaws,
13. but Robin Hood's men were now standing everywhere with their bows and arrows ready.
14. Silently, they disappeared into the forest.

Das Aufgabenblatt eignet sich gut für Partner- oder Gruppenarbeit. Es empfiehlt sich, einige Scheren bereitzuhalten. Die Aufgabe wird leichter, wenn die Schüler die einzelnen Textteile beliebig hin und her verschieben können.

A 19 Morse alphabet

Dies ist eine Konzentrationsaufgabe, die gleichzeitig Tierbezeichnungen wiederholt.
Das Interesse an Tieren ist in der 6. Klasse beachtlich. Selbst unbekannte Tiernamen wecken Neugier und regen zu Fragen an.

1. cat; 2. eagle; 3. rabbit; 4. hedgehog; 5. fish; 6. goose; 7. snake; 8. bird; 9. spider; 10. sheep

A 20 Look for the "odd man out"!

A
1. important; 2. clean; 3. lend; 4. worried; 5. interesting; 6. cruel; 7. wide; 8. important; 9. complete; 10. great

B
1. roll; 2. whisper; 3. ride; 4. shout; 5. break; 6. break; 7. compare; 8. arrest; 9. drive; 10. examine;

C
1. hand; 2. Mark; 3. bird; 4. carrot; 5. New York; 6. computer; 7. garage; 8. school; 9. elephant; 10. fun

A 21 Bingo

Dieses Arbeitsblatt bietet eine Kopiervorlage für Zahlen- und Wortbingo, das bereits in der 5. Klasse in vereinfachter Form beliebt ist und auf verschiedenste Weise verwendet werden kann. Bingo eignet sich zum Wiederholen aller möglichen Formen.

Hier ein Beispiel für *irregular verbs:*
Jeder Schüler füllt alle 16 Felder einer Bingo-Box mit den *past tense*-Formen beliebiger *irregular verbs* aus. z.B.

bent	was	hid	stood
led	meant	rode	began
chose	taught	learnt	won
became	wrote	froze	sold

Die Lehrkraft liest dann in willkürlicher Reihenfolge die Infinitivformen unregelmäßiger Verben vor. Sie unterstreicht dabei – damit die Ergebnisse später überprüft werden können – die bereits erwähnten Verben.
(Hier eine Liste von *irregular verbs: be, beat, become, begin, bend, bet, bite, bleed, blow, break, bring, build, buy, catch, choose, come, cost, cut, do, dream, drink, drive, eat, fall, feed, feel, fight, find, fly, forget, freeze, get, give, go, grow, hang, have, hear, hide, hit, hold, hurt, keep, know, lead, learn, leave, lend, let, lie, lose, make, mean, meet, pay, put, quit, read, ride, ring, rise, run, say, see, sell, send, set, shake, shine, shoot, show, shut, sing, sink, sit, sleep, speak, spell, spend, spread, stand, steal, swim, take, teach, tell, think, throw, understand, wake, wear, win, write*)

Hat ein Schüler / eine Schülerin vier *past tense*-Formen der vorgelesenenVerben in einer Reihe – waagrecht, senkrecht oder diagonal, so ruft er/sie „Bingo!" und hat gewonnen.

Eine Alternative zur Verkürzung eines Durchgangs, da doch recht viele *irregular verbs* existieren: nur Verben bis zum Buchstaben k erlauben, in einem zweiten Durchgang dann die zweite Hälfte des Alphabets einsetzen.
Damit nicht nur Einzelne gewinnen, empfiehlt sich bei mehreren Durchgängen, die Klasse in zwei bis drei Gruppen zu teilen und eine Strichliste der Ergebnisse an der Tafel zu führen.

Weitere Einsatzmöglichkeiten für Bingo:

1. In der 5. Klasse bereits zur Einübung und Wiederholung der Zahlen, auch der Ordnungszahlen. (Zahlenraum vorgeben: z.B. 60–90)
2. Rechnungen; Vorgabe: Zahlen 1–30. Dann aber nicht Zahlen vorlesen, sondern aus jeder Gruppe eine(n) Schüler(in) auswählen, die gemeinsam vom Lehrerpult aus Zahlen anhand von Informationen aus ihrem Lehrbuch abfragen, z.B. "How many days did the Wilsons spend in London?" "What's the number of players in a football match?"
3. Bereits bekannte Jahreszahlen, z.B. 1066, 1666, 1849 und andere Zahlen aus dem Geschichtsunterricht, die dann durch freie Fragen von Mitschülern abgefragt werden.
4. Adverbien - außer Kombinationen mit Adjektiv + *-ly* (*yesterday, tomorrow, often, never, sometimes, always, rarely, seldom, hardly, here, hard ...*)
5. Wörter, die mit Wasser zu tun haben (*wave, spray, ship, swim, dive, drown, seasick, sand, ferry, steamboat, river, lake, Nessie, the Channel Tunnel ...*)
6. Adjektive, die menschliches Verhalten beschreiben (*friendly, nice, polite, terrible, nervous, angry, frightened, furious, nosey, helpful ...*)
7. *Opposites* (*white – black, day – night* usw.; da sehr viele davon existieren, empfiehlt sich ein vorheriges Brainstorming mit Tafelanschrift)
8. Substantive mit unregelmäßigen Pluralen (*men, oxen, thieves, feet, wives, cities, mice, children, teeth, lives, geese, women, deer, fish, sheep ...*)
9. Fahrradteile (*rear light, mudguard, saddle, frame, wheel, handlebar, tyre, bell, front wheel, brakes, chain, gears, pedal, front light*)
10. *Phrasal verbs, buying and selling, auxiliaries, science vocabulary*

...es gibt noch viele Möglichkeiten.

A 22 What's inside?

Prepositions/pronouns
1. for; 2. by; 3. off; 4. their; 5. on; 6. to; 7. in; 8. under; 9. my; 10. down; 11. after; 12. near; 13. into; 14. him; 15. she; 16. he; 17. them; 18. us; 19. her; 20. I; 21. me; 22. at; 23. we; 24. its; 25. you; 26. our; 27. up; 28. they; 29. it; 30. his

Nouns
1. fire; 2. rope; 3. meal; 4. ear; 5. ring; 6. sand; 7. coat; 8. rain; 9. lane; 10. cage; 11. art; 12. ham; 13. lion; 14. son; 15. store; 16. door; 17. key; 18. mice; 19. plan; 20. word; 21. brain; 22. mile; 23. role; 24. deer; 25. string; 26. price; 27. pet; 28. nest; 29. sun; 30. love;

Verbs
1. met; 2. tear; 3. rang; 4. let; 5. say; 6. show; 7. rode; 8. lose; 9. come; 10. make; 11. stay; 12. won; 13. ring; 14. ran; 15. gets; 16. are; 17. win; 18. lost; 19. sat; 20. has; 21. lay; 22. go; 23. came; 24. lost; 25. had; 26. made; 27. fall; 28. fly; 29. eat; 30. ate

A 23 Captions

Für diese Aufgabe werden außer Kopien des Arbeitsblatts auch Schere, Reißnägel oder Klebestreifen für die Wand des Klassenzimmers benötigt.
Die bildgelenkte Arbeit soll den Ideenreichtum der Klasse fördern. Gruppen beliebiger Größe werden gebildet. Jede Gruppe erhält zwei bis drei Kopien des Schülerblatts.
Die Blätter werden in die einzelnen Bilder zerschnitten. Dann suchen die Mitglieder jeder Gruppe eine passende Bildunterschrift bzw. Aussage für die gezeichneten Personen und tragen sie direkt im Bild ein. Da jede Gruppe mehrere Kopien erhalten hat, können auch mehrere Vorschläge eingetragen werden.
Anschließend heften oder kleben die Schüler ihre Ergebnisse, signiert mit einem vorher vereinbarten Kürzel der Gruppe, in willkürlicher Ordnung an eine Wand des Klassenzimmers. Nun dürfen die Texte gelesen werden.
Je nach verbleibender Zeit können zum Abschluss die gelungensten *captions* ermittelt werden. Am einfachsten für die Lehrkraft wäre es, einen Raster an die Tafel zu zeichnen, in dem alle Gruppen mit Kürzel (waagrecht) und alle Bilder (senkrecht) aufgeführt sind. Wenn nun ein Teilnehmer - auch die Lehrkraft - eine Lösung besonders gelungen findet, geht er einfach zur Tafel und macht einen Strich in der entsprechenden Rubrik. Wenn man fünf Lösungen mag, darf man auch fünf Striche machen; es gibt keine Ober- oder Untergrenze. Schüler schätzen solche Freiheiten.

Meist wird zum Abschluss gefragt, wie denn die *captions* im Original lauten. Daher empfiehlt es sich, auch einen Zettel mit dem ursprünglichen Text neben die anderen Lösungen zu hängen. Manche Klassen beziehen auch die Vorlage gern in die Bewertung ein, wobei sie selbst natürlich meist gewinnen!

Die ursprünglichen Sätze lauten im Englischen:
1. "Are you shipwrecked?" - "Yes, why?"
2. "My bar-keeper doesn't understand me ..."

A 24 Finding your own words

1. meal, met, able, (time, table); 2. right, fight, hen, ten, red, feed, fed, Fred, free; 3. hot, hope, liter (AE); lot, ice, lip; 4. make, lake, she, Mike, (milk, shake); 5. lead, made, mode, one, led, lemon; 6. fast, rest, for, eat, fat, forest, east, rat; 7. position, sit, ton, son, tin, post, rest, pin; 8. air, aid, deer, has, had, are, hard, hare, (hair, dress); 9. read, ran, race, bread, bake, red, (break, dance); 10. bull, fall, ball, fill, all, oil, fail; 11. train, net, rain, ran, tan, ring, (enter); 12. vets, able, get, table(s), gee; 13. lose, boss, dress, loose, less; 14. test, rest, ring, testing, net, sing, nest; 15. ring, Kate, tea, sat, sing, song, bang, ate, sea, king, tear, tar, ear; 16. met, meat, rat, pea, ear, tear, pure, (temper); 17. hat, not, nor, tea, rest, nest, test, (north, east); 18. pony, key, Tony, pet, pot, pen, tone, poet; 19. hat, race, hate, care, rate, rat, ate, are; 20. fall, fool, all, tall; 21. cake(s), lake(s), (corn, flakes)

A 25 What a shock!

Aus der Bildgeschichte wird eine Folie für den Overheadprojektor erstellt. Die Klasse wird in Kleingruppen von drei bis vier Schülern aufgeteilt. Die Lehrkraft präsentiert die Bildgeschichte in drei Schritten. Jede Gruppe wird so platziert, dass jeweils nur ein Gruppenmitglied Blick auf den Overheadprojektor hat. Sie/er muss nun den Mitschülern erklären, was auf dem jeweiligen Bildabschnitt zu sehen ist. Dabei sollte sie/er die *past tense*-Formen der angegebenen Verben benutzen.
Natürlich könnte die Bildergeschichte auch in der gewohnten Sitzordnung gemeinsam erarbeitet werden. Erfahrungsgemäß finden Schüler aber an dieser lockeren Form mehr Vergnügen:
Ob es ihm gelungen ist, die angegebenen Verben zu verwenden, wird anschließend von den Partnern überprüft und nicht von der Lehrkraft.

A 26 Birds, cats, horses ...

1. A bird in the hand / is worth / two in the bush.
2. When the cat's / away, the mice / will play.
3. Your bark / is worse than / your bite.
4. Don't kill / the goose that lays / the golden egg.
5. If you pay / peanuts, / you get monkeys.
6. Never look / a gift horse / in the mouth.
7. You can't run / with the hare and / hunt with the hounds.
8. The early / bird / catches the worm.
9. You can't teach / an old dog / new tricks.
10. You may take a horse / to the water, but / you can't / make it drink.
11. One swallow / doesn't make / a summer.
12. Let sleeping / dogs / lie.
13. Fine feathers / make / fine birds.
14. Don't foul / your own / nest.
15. Don't count / your chickens before / they are hatched.
16. Birds / of feather / flock together.

A 27 Intruders

1. happy – nice; 2. question – landing; 3. trainer – speak; 4. listen – understand; 5. bitter – violet; 6. sank – apple; 7. farm – zoo; 8. big – height; 9. taxi – driver; 10. wing - feather; 11. millionaire – lose; 12. meat – chicken; 13. break – see; 14. sugar – giant; 15. fear – horrible; 16. morning – plant; 17. fruit – sweet; 18. other – but; 19. paint – statue; 20. want – has; 21. scandal – advertisement; 22. battery – entrance; 23. drive – tank; 24. three – horizontal; 25. back – into; 26. rocket – jog; 27. doll – camper; 28. guest – amuse; 29. teddy – bed; 30. fitness – suddenly

Vereinzelt sind auch andere Lösungen denkbar, die ebenso anerkannt werden können, wenn sie logisch begründet werden.

A 28 Letter puzzle

1. enjoy; 2. disappeared; 3. chemical; 4. ambulance; 5. understood; 6. decision; 7. appendix; 8. encourage; 9. familiar; 10. friendly; 11. introduce; 12. photography; 13. nationality; 14. population; 15. challenge; 16. secretary; 17. careless; 18. Halloween; 19. colourful; 20. divorced; 21. scientist; 22. landscape; 23. injure; 24. lightning; 25. scrapbook; 26. terminal; 27. husband; 28. instead; 29. customs; 30. lawyer; 31. persuade; 32. century; 33. questionnaire; 34. pineapple; 35. rehearse; 36. hovercraft; 37. several; 38. everywhere; 39. businessman; 40. doughnut; 41. earthquake; 42. fisherman; 43. breakdance; 44. especially; 45. girlfriend; 46. European; 47. loudspeaker; 48. immediately

A 29 Quintet

A

1. *food:* fish and chips, carrot, vegetables, tea, ham; 2. *crime:* policeman, catch, prison, thief, steal; 3. *question words:* why, how old, where, what, who; 4. *feeling:* afraid, nervous, happy, curious, angry; 5. *music:* concert, player, listen, piano, jazz;

B

1. *fire:* alarm bell, siren, rescue, burn, fireman; 2. *summertime:* swimming-pool, holidays, ice-cream, sunglasses, sea; 3. *farm:* pig, milking, farmhand, hen, feed; 4. *weather:* degrees, cloudy, thunderstorm, fog, lightning; 5. *cowboy:* Stetson hat, Texas, cow herds, ride, campfire;

C

1. *newspaper:* editor, ad, news, reporter, sports page; 2. *hospital:* nurse, visitor, doctor, operation, patient; 3. *seaside:* sand, wave, seagull, fishing boats, dune; 4. *sightseeing:* coach, famous building, guide, museum, camera; 5. *California:* Hollywood, Silicon Valley, giant redwoods, Gold Rush, Death Valley

A 30 Towns/countries

Das Spiel „Stadt-Land-Fluss" ist ein altbekannter Dauerbrenner bei unseren Schülern. Warum nicht auch einmal in Englisch? Im ersten Lernjahr ist noch zu wenig Vokabular vorhanden, doch kann man es bereits im dritten, in manchen Klassen schon in der zweiten Hälfte des zweiten Lernjahres einsetzen.
Die Vorgehensweise ist einfach. Man spielt in Gruppen von zwei bis sechs Schülern. Eine Person sagt im Geiste das Alphabet auf. An irgendeiner Stelle wird sie von anderen Gruppenmitgliedern unterbrochen. Mit dem damit getroffenen Buchstaben versuchen nun alle Teilnehmer Städte-, Ländernamen usw. zu finden. Dann wird ausgewertet. Für jedes richtige Wort – d.h., korrekt geschrieben und auch wirklich existierend – bekommt jeder Spieler fünf Punkte. Zehn Punkte erhält man für Worte, die kein anderes Mitglied der Gruppe vorweisen kann. Die *credits* werden zusammengezählt und rechts notiert. Dann beginnt der / die Nächste mit der Aufzählung des Alphabets. Die Rubriken „Fluss" und „Pflanze" wurden durch andere Ausdrücke ersetzt, die sich für den Englischunterricht besser eignen. Man könnte aber jederzeit zur Wiederholung bestimmter Begriffe eine Überschrift ändern, z.B. in *irregular verbs, tools, adjectives of nationality* o.ä.

A 31 Hidden sentences

1. How are you?
2. Let us go by train./Let us go and ring.
3. Can I help you?
4. He used to live in the city.
5. What did I say?
6. His son was reading.
7. He left it in the car.
8. One story was the best of all.
9. There were bears in the forest.
10. She paid the bill.
11. My aunt sent me a card.
12. Dan liked talking to her.
13. Can I see the room now?
14. What do they eat?

Diese Aufgabe wird von Schülern unterschiedlich schnell bewältigt. Bei auftretenden Schwierigkeiten könnte der Inhalt des jeweils nächsten Satzes von der Lehrkraft umschrieben werden, bevor ihn die Gruppe zu entziffern versucht.
Mitunter kommen die Schüler auch auf neue, überraschende Lösungen. Solange sie logisch zu begründen sind, sollte man sie gelten lassen.

A 32 Taboo

Für dieses Spiel wird das Arbeitsblatt entlang der gestrichelten Linien zu Zetteln geschnitten. Es werden zwei Gruppen gebildet, von denen jede einen versteckten Stapel Zettel erhält. (Die Lehrkraft sollte ein vollständiges Aufgabenblatt für sich kopieren, damit sie den Überblick behält.)
Innerhalb einer vereinbarten Zeit (z.B. 1 – 3 Minuten) deckt nun ein Mitglied der Gruppe nach dem anderen je eine Karte auf und versucht, das Wort der eigenen Gruppe zu erklären, aber ohne die darunter aufgeführten Begriffe zu verwenden. Die Lehrkraft oder ein zuvor ernannter *director* aus der Klasse sieht ihm dabei zur Kontrolle über die Schulter.
Wer glaubt, den Begriff zu erraten, ruft ihn dem erklärenden Schüler zu. (Ständiges lautes Zurufen ebbt meist nach kurzer Zeit ab, weil dadurch weitere Erklärungen erschwert werden und Zeit verloren geht.)
Errät die Gruppe den ersten Begriff innerhalb der vereinbarten Zeit, bekommt sie die Karte und der nächste Schüler kann schnell eine weitere Karte umdrehen und den nächsten Begriff erklären. Nicht vollständig erratene Karten verfallen nach Ablauf der Zeit.
Wird ein „verbotener" Ausdruck zur Erklärung verwendet, unterbricht die Lehrkraft/der *director* (Pfeifchen oder quietschende Gegenstände eignen sich hierfür gut und erhöhen die Spannung) und die Karte geht in den Besitz der gegnerischen Gruppe über. Gesten, deutsche Ausdrücke und Lautmalerei sind ebenfalls nicht erlaubt. Auch das gesuchte Wort oder Teile davon (wie etwa bei *baby brother* die Ausdrücke *baby* oder *brother*) dürfen nicht in der Erklärung erwähnt werden.
Die Gruppe, welche am Schluss die meisten Karten besitzt, gewinnt. Das Spiel endet wahlweise, wenn jeder Schüler einen Begriff erklärt hat oder 2 Minuten vor dem Gongschlag oder wenn keine Karten mehr zur Verfügung stehen.
Sollte das Spiel gut angekommen sein, kann es zu einem späteren Zeitpunkt mit anderen Karten und noch aktiverer Schülerbeteiligung wiederholt werden:

1. Es werden Gruppen gebildet (je 2 – 3 Schüler).
2. Jeder Schüler sucht aus seinem Lehrbuch ein Wort heraus, das ihm der oder die Partner in der Fremdsprache erklären sollen.
3. Nun erstellt jeder Schüler eine Karte nach vorliegendem Muster, wobei drei Ausdrücke als „verboten" notiert werden.

Anschließend werden zwei oder mehr große Gruppen gebildet. Dabei ist darauf zu achten, dass Partner aus Zweier- /Dreiergruppen auch beim endgültigen Spiel in derselben Gruppe bleiben, damit sie ihre Kenntnisse nicht verraten.
Auf diese Weise kann z.B. der Wortschatz von zwei bis drei beliebigen Lektionen eines Lehrbuchs spielerisch wiederholt werden.

„Taboo" ermöglicht vielfältige Formen des Spielablaufs und der Gruppenbildung. Mehrere Gruppen von je sechs bis acht Personen werden gebildet (gerade Zahl!), diese in A und B aufgeteilt und so im Kreis um einen Tisch gesetzt, dass A neben B und diese(r) wiederum neben A sitzt usw. Alle Karten von A und B werden zusammengemischt und verdeckt auf einen Stapel gelegt.
Nun beginnt ein Mitglied der A-Gruppe. Es deckt das erste Blatt auf und umschreibt den entsprechenden Begriff, wobei ihm die beiden rechts und links von ihm sitzenden B-Mitschüler zur Kontrolle in die Karten sehen. Nur Mitglieder der A-Gruppe raten jetzt mit. Keine Karte darf weggelegt werden, ohne dass der Begriff erraten worden ist, sonst ist sie an die gegnerische Gruppe verloren.
Anschließend wird der ganze Reststapel verdeckt an den Nachbarn / die Nachbarin weitergereicht, der bzw. die für die B-Gruppe nun einen oder mehrere Begriffe vorstellt.

A 33 Towns and cities

Die Übung ist geeignet ab dem 4. Lernjahr. Es können auch Landkarten über England und Amerika (meist in den Lehrbüchern auf der Umschlaginnenseite abgedruckt) hinzugezogen werden.

British

1. Manchester; 2. Glasgow; 3. London; 4. Cambridge; 5. Brighton; 6. Aberdeen; 7. Liverpool; 8. Oxford; 9. Scarborough; 10. Windsor; 11. Aberystwyth; 12. Edinburgh; 13. Swansea; 14. Belfast; 15. Whitby; 16. Canterbury; 17. Portsmouth; 18. Bournemouth; 19. Folkestone; 20. Dover;

American

1. New York; 2. Oklahoma City; 3. Detroit; 4. Boston; 5. Houston; 6. San Francisco; 7. Los Angeles; 8. New Orleans; 9. Kansas City; 10. Hollywood; 11. Toronto; 12. Memphis; 13. Washington; 14. Philadelphia; 15. Salt Lake City; 16. Baltimore; 17. Chicago; 18. Las Vegas; 19. Cleveland; 20. Nashville

A 34 What's my job?

Dieses Spiel eignet sich hervorragend zur Wiederholung und zum Üben von Fragesätzen.

A 35 Animal idioms

1. ein Elefant im Porzellanladen
2. der Tropfen, der das Fass zum Überlaufen bringt
3. (jd.) könnte kein Wässerchen trüben
4. pudelnass aussehen
5. eng zusammengepfercht
6. sehr zufrieden aussehen
7. Lampenfieber haben
8. kopflos herumrennen
9. zwei Fliegen mit einer Klappe schlagen
10. Probleme verursachen
11. ein Versager sein
12. eine übereifrige Person
13. erst einmal abwarten
14. den Stier bei den Hörnern packen
15. die Katze aus dem Sack lassen
16. keine Wirkung haben (an jdm. abperlen)
17. grinsen wie einHonigkuchenpferd
18. übel gelaunt sein
19. rennen wie ein geölter Blitz

A 36 Tippling or prutting?

Diese Aufgabe findet bereits bei kreativen 7. Klassen Anklang. Die Klasse wird in Gruppen bis höchstens jeweils vier Teilnehmer (damit sich wirklich alle Gruppenmitglieder beteiligen können) aufgeteilt. Manche Schüler sind allein kreativer, daher könnte man zur Abwechslung einmal die Wahl der Gruppengröße bis zur erwähnten Obergrenze völlig den Schülern überlassen. Jede Gruppe versucht die Bedeutung der kodierten Verben zu erraten und erhält nach einer vorgegebenen Zeit Gelegenheit, ihre Lösung vorzutragen. Kleinere Veränderungen des Textes sind erlaubt. Anschließend wird die Originalgeschichte vorgelesen, sofern sie nicht bereits zuvor erraten wurde. Bleibt noch Zeit, können die Schüler selbst eine Geschichte erfinden und aufschreiben, in der Schlüssel- durch Nonsensewörter ersetzt werden.

tipple: *play*	arnt: *stop*
frish: *begin*	colth: *wash*
shrit/shrot: *do/did*	crite: *break*
brubble: *cry*	bod/bede/bo: *was/were/are*
plup: *ask*	gose: *go*
strune: *cook*	wock: *say*
prut: *hit*	trose: *clean*
flit: *had*	

Mrs Peters had two children. Sammy was seven years old, and his sister Annie was four. Sammy went to school, but Annie didn't. When Sammy was at home, he often played with Annie while their mother was cooking or washing or cleaning, and he was usually very nice to his small sister and didn't hit her or break anything, and Mrs Peters was free to do her work quietly.
One Saturday morning, the two children were playing in the garden while their mother was cooking dinner. They were quite happy until Annie suddenly began to cry and went into the kitchen to her mother.
Mrs Peters stopped cooking and said, "Why are you crying, Annie?"
"Sammy's broken my toy horse," Annie said, crying more loudly.
"How did he break it?" her mother asked.
Annie stopped crying, but did not answer for a few seconds. Then she said, "I hit him on the head with it."

Leicht geändert aus: L. A. Hill, Elementary Steps to Understanding. Oxford: OUP 1980, p. 32

A 37 What goes together?

1. good as new
2. as easy as falling off a log
3. quick as lightning

4. stubborn as a mule
5. thin as a stick
6. live like a king
7. hot as hell
8. quiet as a mouse
9. I know it like the back of my hand
10. feel like a million dollars
11. cold as ice
12. it runs like clockwork
13. drunk as a skunk
14. clear as crystal
15. dull as dishwater
16. He's hard as nails
17. rich as Croesus
18. red as a beetroot
19. pleased as a punch
20. green as grass
21. laugh like a drain
22. free as the air
23. drop sth. like a hot brick
24. dry as dust
25. safe as houses

A 38 It's your choice

1. journey; 2. perhaps; 3. port; 4. wealthy; 5. to open; 6. timid; 7. tune; 8. ill; 9. worry; 10. impressing; 11. confidence; 12. understandable; 13. wild; 14. kind; 15. smart; 16. price; 17. diciton-ary; 18. irregular; 19. opinion; 20. once; 21. show; 22. to fasten; 23. understanding; 24. more; 25. to like; 26. closely; 27. path; 28. guard; 29. education; 30. influence

A 39 Opposite pairs

1. nephew – uncle; 2. the Statue of Liberty – Big Ben; 3. remember – forget; 4. guess - know; 5. ceiling – floor; 6. dessert – starter; 7. murderer – victim; 8. leave – arrive; 9. different - similar; 10. shout – whisper; 11. exit – entrance; 12. great – awful; 13. beautiful – ugly; 14. cry – laugh; 15. together - alone; 16. boring – exciting; 17. straighten – bend; 18. destroy – build

A 40 Word acrobatics

Hier einige Lösungsvorschläge für den Fall, dass hartnäckig behauptet wird, mit einer dieser Buchstabenkombinationen gäbe es keine Lösung:

	Noun	*Verb*	*Adjective*
1.	starter	stay	satisfied
2.	journey	renovate	wrong
3.	language	sang	general
4.	bed	bleed	bearded
5.	butter	turn	true
6.	law	walk	awful
7.	yoghurt	worry	royal
8.	interest	whispered	expensive
9.	change	caught	characteristic
10.	friend	find	fantastic
11.	headmaster	made	dangerous
12.	holidays	stay	easy
13.	dice	cried	delicious
14.	gentleman	mean	normal
15.	boot	misunderstood	opposite
16.	chapter	panic	practical
17.	raincoat	organize	official
18.	leaflet	flew	useful
19.	year	carry	angry
20.	guitar	guard	unchanged

A 41 Word cascades

FIND	RULE	STORY	MARK
BIND	ROLE	STORE	BARK
BAND	ROSE	STARE	BARN
BANK	LOSE	SHARE	EARN
FAST	WOKE	FORM	COME
LAST	WAKE	FORK	CAME
LIST	MAKE	WORK	SAME
LIFT	MADE	WORD	SAFE
SIDE	TAKE	SINK	POEM
RIDE	WAKE	SANK	POET
RISE	WAVE	SAND	POST
RISK	GAVE	BAND	PAST
LIKE	BOAT	MUST	HOME
BIKE	BEAT	MOST	HOPE
BITE	BEAR	LOST	ROPE
KITE	TEAR	LOSE	ROLE
MAD	SKIRT	WELL	GANG
SAD	SHIRT	WALL	SANG
SAT	SHORT	WALK	SING
EAT	SHOUT	TALK	KING
LOVE	DUCK	MIND	LINK
LIVE	LUCK	MINE	LINE
GIVE	LOCK	MILE	FINE
GAVE	SOCK	MILD	FIND
WAVE	SICK	MILK	KIND
MEAL			
MEAT			
BEAT			
SEAT			
HEAT			

A 42 The latest horror story

Die Klasse wird in Gruppen von 4–5 Schülern aufgeteilt. Jede Gruppe erhält einen Streifen mit vier Nomen, die sie in ihrer Horrorgeschichte einbauen muss. Normalerweise sind die Schüler sehr erfinderisch bei dieser Art Wettbewerb. Auch hier sollte man großzügig sein und auch abenteuerliche Lösungen akzeptieren.

Nach einer Arbeitsphase von ca. 25–30 Minuten werden die einzelnen Gruppen aufgefordert, ihre Geschichten vorzulesen. Die anderen Gruppen müssen raten, welche Begriffe vorgegeben waren und verwendet werden mussten. Gewinner ist die Gruppe, die ihre Begriffe so geschickt einzubauen wusste, dass möglichst wenig erraten wurden.

A 43 Creativity center

1. liar, lion, loaf, carol, for, coal, oil
2. nice, tone, note, count
3. nest, mine, name, neat, mist, meat, same, tame, some, sonnet
4. sank, arks, rank, Kansas, ran
5. seen, teens, sent, nest, sets, sees
6. that, hat, tout, host, toast
7. women, come, mine, wise, mice, nice
8. sons, sins, wins
9. hint, clan, train, colt, torn
10. same, masses, tastes, chases, tame, sets, must, such, messes
11. hands, ladder, roads, Nile, real, seal, sold, holds, landed, sand, land, Neil, horse, leads, reads, nails, sailed, handles
12. deer, dear, read, lead, ward
13. wins, harm, spin, here, hears, pears, spares, names, mine, hers, wasp, whisper, news, means, amen, same, warm, wars
14. hang
15. virgin, rain, gain
16. sting, wing, sang, ghost, night, waist, sigh, saint, hint
17. gone
18. many, madly, (Mary, land)
19. note, tone, vote, (venom)
20. Alan, nails, sail, soul

A 44 Eye and mouth – ear and hand

An Arbeitsmaterial wird die Bildvorlage in Form einer Folie und ein Overheadprojektor benötigt.

Die Schüler arbeiten in Zweiergruppen.

Ein Partner sitzt mit dem Rücken zur Projektionsfläche, der andere bekommt den Auftrag, alle Bildteile, die nachher gezeigt werden, möglichst genau zu beschreiben, so dass sein Partner davon eine Zeichnung anfertigen kann.

Nun zeigt die Lehrkraft das erste Bild – in Etappen. Zunächst wird der linke Teil aufgedeckt; man sieht die Mütze im Gras liegen. Dann wird nach und nach der Rest des ersten Bildes „enthüllt", zuletzt die verbogenen Fahrräder.

Mit dem zweiten Bild wird – nach Partnerwechsel – genauso verfahren.

A 45 What on earth is that?

1. the ins and outs
2. a thick skin
3. a snow job
4. a place in the sun
5. a heart of gold
6. forbidden fruit
7. a blind spot
8. tall tales
9. a frog in your throat
10. small potatoes
11. a red herring
12. a feeding frenzy
13. the tip of the iceberg
14. the whys and wherefores
15. red tape
16. a pain in the neck
17. a false dawn

A 46 Concentration!

◇ clever, wealthy, peaceful

▭ disgusting, industrial, sensible

○ successful, actual

□ mysterious, ridiculous

⏢ favourite, serious

△ horrified, unemployed

▢ incredible, extraordinary

▽ abstract, alive

⬯ awful, available, foreign

⬭ cruel, delicious, accurate

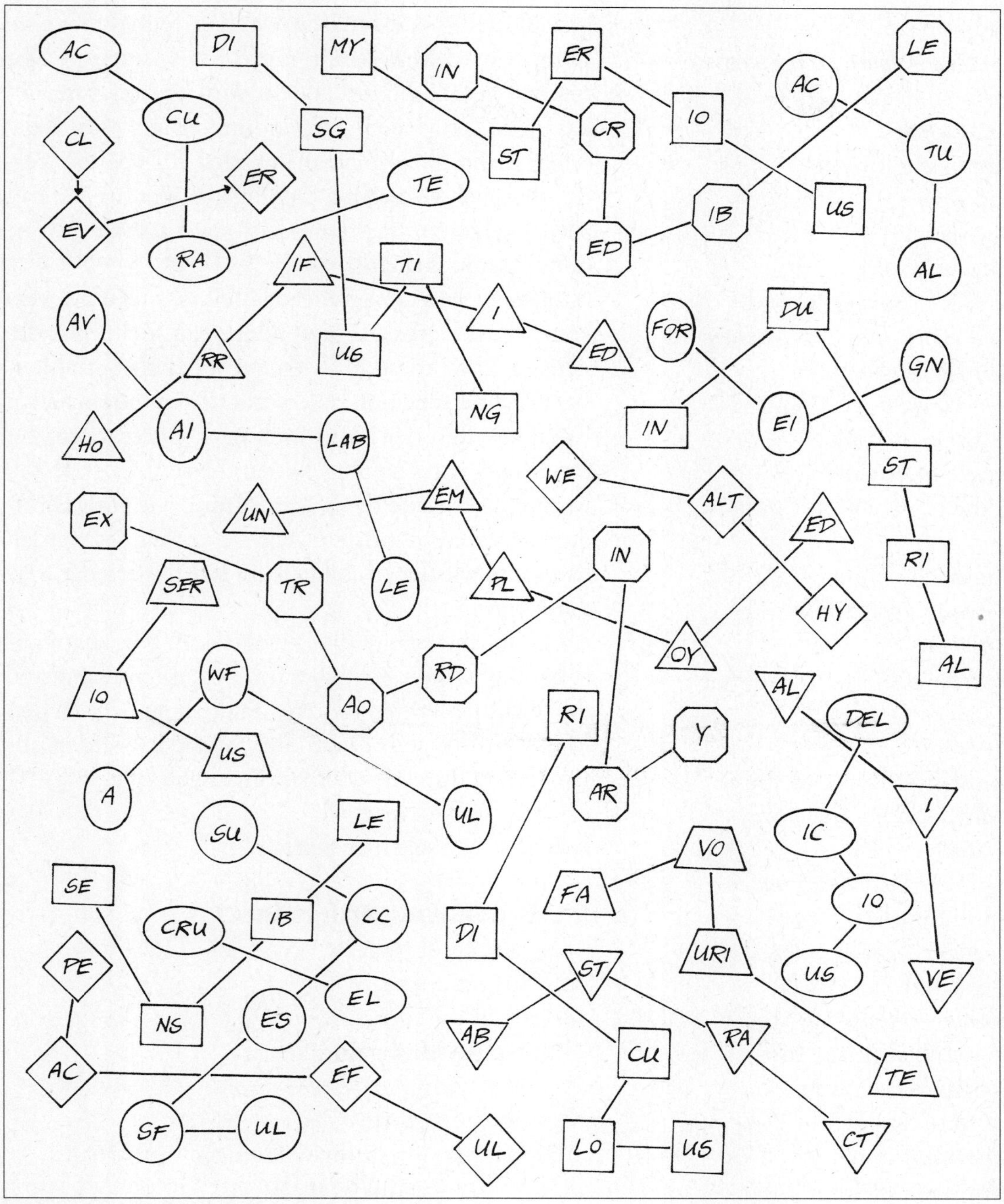

A 47 Opposites

1. death; 2. freedom; 3. to close; 4. ashamed; 5. to forbid; 6. nevertheless; 7. pleased; 8. to leave; 9. children; 10. to be born; 11. selfish; 12. to accept; 13. at once; 14. to export; 15. seldom; 16. solution; 17. to fail; 18. urban; 19. to receive; 20. answer; 21. to love; 22. smart; 23. to fall asleep; 24. disappointment; 25. peace; 26. detective; 27. stupidity; 28. to abolish; 29. true; 30. private; 31. unimportant; 32. heaven; 33. effect; 34. path; 35. the indiviual; 36. friend; 37. exciting; 38. civilization; 39. to divorce; 40. wealthy; 41. friendly; 42. aggressive; 43. healthy; 44. breakfast; 45. to drive out; 46. ridiculous

A 48 Idiomatic expressions?

1. Qh to catch someone's eye
jdn. auf sich aufmerksam machen
2. Tz to make ends meet
gerade mit seinem Geld auskommen
3. Fq to cut a long story short
kurz und gut
4. Wl to take many years
viele Jahre dauern
5. Oa to be faced with a problem
mit einem Problem konfrontiert sein
6. Lc to take sth. for granted
etwas als selbstverständlich voraussetzen
7. At to hit sb. in the eye
offensichtlich sein
8. Zn to drop s.o. a line
jdm. ein paar Zeilen schreiben

9. Bw to get a jump on s.o.
jemandem einen Schritt voraus sein
10. Du to get one's own back on sb.
sich an jdm. rächen
11. Jr to have a lot going for one
viele Vorteile haben
12. Hy to put up with sth.
sich mit etwas abfinden
13. Cj to keep one's feet on the ground
auf dem Boden der Tatsachen bleiben
14. Ve to shoot yourself in the foot
ein Eigentor schießen
15. Sg to be into sth.
sich für etwas interessieren
16. Yo to step on the gas
Gas geben
17. Is to be dying for the holidays
die Ferien kaum abwarten können
18. Ed to get the picture
etwas begreifen
19. Kb to do well
Erfolg haben
20. Mx to look on the bright side of sth.
etwas von der positiven Seite sehen
21. Gm to be in charge
die Leitung (Verantwortung) haben
22. Xi to be taken in by sth.
auf etwas hereinfallen
23. Nf to get out of hand
außer Kontrolle geraten
24. Rp to take the rough with the smooth
das Leben nehmen, wie es ist
25. Uk to get worked up about sth.
sich über etwas aufregen
26. Pv to take a dim view of sth.
etwas missbilligen

A 49 Misfits

1. unfriendly; 2. sick; 3. law; 4. impression; 5. awful; 6. to cover; 7. Chaplin; 8. electronics; 9. autumn; 10. USA; 11. to ask; 12. to carry; 13. teacher; 14. lunch; 15. basket; 16. Thames; 17. back; 18. president; 19. taxes; 20. next year; 21. to obey; 22. Sioux; 23. penfriend; 24. agency; 25. it's

A 50 Buy my invention!

Ein ausgeprägter Hang zu Blödeleien lässt sich in der heutigen Schülergeneration erkennen. Warum diese Neigung nicht für den Sprachunterricht nützen?
Je nach Zeit bilden die Schüler eine beliebige Anzahl Gruppen. (Je mehr Gruppen es gibt, desto länger dauert die Präsentation. Allerdings steigt erfahrungsgemäß die Produktivität, je weniger Teilnehmer eine Gruppe hat.) Man benötigt pro Klasse nur eine Kopie des Schülerblattes. Diese wird so zerschnitten, dass jede Gruppe eine Erfindung erhält. (Die Vorschläge, die übrig bleiben, werden für spätere Verwendung, einen zweiten Durchgang oder für den Fall zurückgehalten, dass einer Gruppe zu ihrer „Erfindung" gar nichts einfällt.)
Nun versuchen die Schüler, als Teilnehmer eines Verkaufswettbewerbs, Argumente zu sammeln, mit denen sie „ihr Produkt" in einem möglichst strahlendem Licht erscheinen lassen und so dem potenziellen Käufer (= Rest der Klasse) schmackhaft machen.
Innerhalb eines vorgegebenen Zeitraums (z.B. 15 Minuten) entscheidet jede Gruppe, wie ihre Erfindung überhaupt aussieht, wie sie verwendet werden kann und wie der „Käufer" zum Kauf überredet werden kann.
Anschließend erfolgt die Präsentation. Wie zuvor angekündigt wurde, gelingt es nur den überzeugendsten drei Gruppen, ihre Produkte an die Frau bzw. an den Mann zu bringen. Diese drei Gruppen werden abschließend durch Akklamation ausgewählt.

A 51 siehe nächste Seite

A 52 Who on earth is that?

1. a jack of all trades
2. a sitting duck
3. part of the furniture
4. the piggy in the middle
5. a busybody
6. a port in a storm
7. a voice crying in the wilderness
8. a nodding acquaintance
9. a night owl
10. a shrinking violet
11. the apple of your eye
12. a couch potato
13. a knight in shining armour
14. the big guns
15. a tough cookie

A 53 Starry wor(l)ds

A: of, go, tin, get, fog, ring, wing, worn, frog, wire, grown, winter, getting, forgetting

B: or, day, and, nor, pay, gun, rap, girl, liar, nail, play, roar, land, plan, groan, round, ground, playground

C: ran, ice, ear, led, and, lice, land, dead, Sean, lied, lead, lady, rare, lean, rail, clear, rally, silly, sends, lanes, slice, Daisy, clean, daily, crane, really, raises

A 51 The double meaning tower

1.	C	U	P					
2.	T	I	E					
3.	L	I	E					
4.	R	U	N					
5.	F	A	L	L				
6.	C	A	S	E				
7.	F	O	O	T				
8.	P	A	R	T				
9.	F	I	N	E				
10.	R	I	N	G				
11.	D	U	C	K				
12.	R	O	L	L				
13.	W	O	R	K				
14.	P	L	U	G				
15.	R	A	C	E				
16.	M	I	N	D				
17.	B	E	A	R				
18.	P	A	R	K				
19.	B	A	T	H				
20.	B	I	L	L				
21.	D	A	T	E				
22.	R	I	G	H	T			
23.	C	L	O	S	E			
24.	F	L	O	O	R			
25.	P	L	A	N	T			
26.	R	E	C	O	R	D		
27.	V	I	O	L	E	T		
28.	C	O	U	N	T	E	R	
29.	G	E	N	E	R	A	L	
30.	P	R	A	C	T	I	C	E

D: pin, oil, sea, sins, leap, nose, peas, lies, none, pins, sane, pole, apple, piles, noise, people, please, opinion, nonsense, pineapples

E: war, end, raw, dare, dear, draw, news, read, near, rear, road, send(er), ended, warden, opened, depended, dangerous

F: bit, had, hit, his, set, sit, tag, then, bind, thin, ties, bites, high(t), tight, eight, hands, thing, dishes, behind, binding, hanging, singing, hesitate

A 54 Body idioms

1. skeleton (to have a skeleton in the cupboard/closet: *etwas zu verbergen haben*)
2. teeth (armed to the teeth: *bis an die Zähne bewaffnet*)
3. necks (to breathe down someone's neck: *jemanden genauestens kontrollieren*)
4. skin, teeth (to do sth. by the skin of your teeth: *etwas sehr knapp schaffen, um Haaresbreite nicht erreichen*)
5. face to face (*von Angesicht zu Angesicht*)
6. flesh (to make somebody's flesh creep or crawl, to make somebody's skin crawl: *jemandem eine Gänsehaut verursachen*)
7. tongue, cheek (sth. is said or written tongue in cheek: *nicht ernst gemeint*)
8. foot (to have to foot the bill: *etwas bezahlen müssen, d.h., „seinen Namen an den Fuß der Rechnung setzen müssen"*)
9. blood (There is bad blood between two people / groups: *es gibt böses Blut zwischen zwei Personen/ Gruppen*)
10. heart (to set your heart on something: *etwas unbedingt wollen*)
11. nose (to keep one's nose to the grindstone: *Hart arbeiten und sich um nichts anderes kümmern*)
12. hairs (to have somebody by the short hairs/by the short and curlies: *jemanden vollständig in der Hand haben*)
13. bone (to have a bone to pick with someone: *mit jemandem ein Hühnchen zu rupfen haben*)

A 55 The US States: test your memory

Diese Konzentrationsaufgabe könnte auch bereits in einer 9. oder einer interessierten 8. Klasse eingesetzt werden. Als Arbeitsmittel sind erforderlich Kopien des Arbeitsblattes für die Klasse, Overheadprojektor sowie eine Folienkopie des Lösungsblattes. Um den üblichen Drang, vom Nachbarn abzuschreiben, von vorneherein auszuschalten, sollte der Klasse vor Beginn der Übung Gelegenheit gegeben werden, die

Arbeitsanweisung vollständig zu lesen. In einem ersten Schritt wird zunächst reines Wissen abgefragt. Die Schüler versuchen möglichst viele ihnen bereits bekannte Staaten einzutragen. Wenn dies zuvor vereinbart wurde, kann auch in Zweiergruppen gearbeitet werden, um den Wettbewerbscharakter der Übung abzuschwächen. Auch bei oft mageren Ergebnissen – manche Schüler können nicht mehr als drei Bundesstaaten korrekt benennen – sollte hier keine Kritik erfolgen, da nicht Sachwissen, sondern Merkfähigkeit überprüft werden soll. Zudem lernen auch schwache Schüler im Verlauf der Übung die Lage etlicher Staaten hinzu. Als Nächstes vergleicht der Schüler seine Ergebnisse mit der Lösungsfolie, die von der Lehrkraft aufgelegt wird. Wichtig ist, dass er sich selbst beurteilt und dadurch auch bei schwachen Ergebnissen nicht zum Abschreiben verleitet wird. Dann erfolgt die Konzentrationsphase, bei der die Schüler sich möglichst viele Staaten einprägen sollten. Für die Konzentrationsphase können ein bis drei Minuten gewährt werden.
Beim anschließenden Vergleich der Ergebnisse sollte völlig auf Kontrolle durch die Lehrkraft verzichtet werden. Regen Sie die Schüler zum internen Vergleich mit Mitschülern ihrer Wahl an und erlauben Sie ihnen, zu diesem Zweck kurz im Klassenzimmer herumzugehen.
Statt *"How many credits did you get?"* weckt sicherlich die Frage *"Do you like your results?"* eher das Mitteilungsbedürfnis Ihrer Klasse.

A 56 In one word

1. buildings; 2. vegetables; 3. jobs; 4. modal auxiliaries 5. weight; 6. politicians; 7. behaviour; 8. doors; 9. writers; 10. insects; 11. prepositions of place; 12. bicycle parts; 13. working places; 14. parking; 15. to judge; 16. stories; 17. hunters; 18. Civil War; 19. instruments; 20. capitals 21. public transport; 22. sounds; 23. footwear; 24. money; 25. illness; 26. to kill; 27. space travel; 28. seasons; 29. computer; 30. sizes; 31. fruit; 32. vehicles; 33. relatives; 34. plates and dishes; 35. food; 36. crew members; 37. weather; 38. rivers; 39. drinks; 40. furniture

A 57 American English – British English

American English	British English
1. bill	banknote
2. allowance	pocket money
3. movie	film
4. can	tin
5. elective	optional subject
6. garbage	rubbish
7. subway	underground
8. attorney	lawyer
9. guy	chap
10. sidewalk	pavement
11. mailbox	letterbox
12. emergency room	casualty department
13. check	cheque
14. pants	trousers
15. backyard	back garden
16. plow	plough
17. rooster	cock
18. soda (coll.)	lemonade
19. trunk	boot
20. requirement	compulsory subject
21. fall	autumn
22. candy	sweet
23. downtown	in the centre
24. rummage sale	jumble sale
25. apartment	flat
26. corn	maize
27. store	shop
28. gas	petrol
29. student	pupil
30. janitor	caretaker
31. truck	lorry
32. vacation	holidays
33. rubber boot	wellington
34. to guess	to suppose

A 58 Compounds

1. power cut
   power station
   power-sharing
   power plant
2. top speed
   speedometer
   speed trap
   speed limit
3. air-conditioning
   airport
   open air
   aircraft
4. food poisoning
   junk food
   food-chain
   dog food
5. handwriting
   handicraft
   minute-hand
   farmhand
6. boarding school
   school-bag
   schoolyard
   school uniform
7. overlook
   good-looking
   lookout
   looking-glass
8. farmhouse
   health farm
   farmyard
   diary farm
9. playground
   role play
   playboy
   playing card
10. hunting-ground
    job hunt(er)
    huntsman
    bargain-hunting

11. postman
    postcard
    post office
    post-free

12. board game
    gamekeeper
    team game
    games teacher

13. shifting sand
    sandman
    sand-dune
    sandpaper

14. cry-baby
    baby boom
    babysit
    baby-talk

15. railcard
    handrail
    railway
    railroad

16. set-aside
    TV set
    set-up
    jet set

A 59 Combinations

1. Wh a lot - plenty - sufficient
2. Lt perfect - ideal - most suitable
3. Jn to last - to continue - to remain
4. Kr busy - occupied - active
5. Pj gradually - slowly - by degrees
6. Qd to trouble - to worry - to bother
7. Rz happy - satisfied - pleased
8. Oy certain - sure - beyond doubt
9. Te at once - immediately - without delay
10. Bo to talk - to chat - to converse
11. Sg to get - to receive - to obtain
12. As profound - deep - intense
13. Xi to injure - to hurt - to harm
14. Dv correct - accurate - true
15. Cp to show - to point out - to indicate
16. Ul good - acceptable - of high quality
17. Gu to suppose - to guess - to assume
18. Zc remarkable – unusual – exceptional
19. Ew detail - aspect - small part
20. Fx to take away - to remove - to get rid of
21. Mb initially - at the beginning - first
22. Yf kind - friendly - amiable
23. Im usually - in general - mainly
24. Nq fairly - pretty - rather
25. Vk constant - never changing - invariable
26. Ha to be interested in - to be keen on - to be fond of

A 60 The unicorn puzzle

Die Schüler erhalten eine Kopie der *scrambled story* und sollen die Zeilen ausschneiden und in die richtige Reihenfolge bringen. (Vollständiger Text siehe nächste Seite!)
Die meisten Schüler erledigen gerne Arbeitsaufträge in Gruppen, bei denen der Einzelne nicht so unter Leistungszwang steht wie in der traditionellen Klassensituation. Es empfiehlt sich daher, die Klasse in beliebig viele Gruppen aufzuteilen, die so klein gehalten sind, dass jedes Mitglied auf die Streifchen sehen kann. Gewonnen hat die Gruppe, die den Text als erste richtig zusammengesetzt hat.

Die Geschichte kann je nach Wunsch anschließend eingehender besprochen werden. Der Wortschatz kann vor oder während der Gruppenarbeit erklärt werden. Man könnte aber auch das Gegenteil versuchen: nachdem der Text gemeinsam laut gelesen wurde, lässt sich die Lehrkraft von der Klasse die folgenden Begriffe erklären bzw. aus dem Kontext erschließen:

to crop - a unicorn - mythical - a tulip - gravely - to rouse - a booby - the booby-hatch - the fore-head - a gloat - a strait-jacket - to leap - to seize - to subdue - to curse - an institution - ever after.

Once upon a sunny morning a man who sat in a breakfast nook looked up from his scrambled eggs to see a white unicorn with a golden horn quietly cropping the roses in the garden. The man went up to the bedroom where his wife was still asleep and woke her. 'There's a unicorn in the garden,' he said. 'Eating roses.' She opened one unfriendly eye and looked at him. 'The unicorn is a mythical beast,' she said, and turned her back on him. The man walked slowly downstairs and out into the garden. The unicorn was still there; he was now browsing among the tulips. 'Here, unicorn,' said the man, and he pulled up a lily and gave it to him. The unicorn ate it gravely. With a high heart, because there was a unicorn in his garden, the man went upstairs and roused his wife again. 'The unicorn,' he said, 'ate a lily.' His wife sat up in bed and looked at him, coldly. 'You are a booby,' she said, 'and I am going to have you put in the booby-hatch.' The man, who had never liked the words 'booby' and 'booby-hatch', and who liked them even less on a shining morning when there was a unicorn in the garden, thought for a moment. 'We'll see about that,' he said. He walked over to the door. 'He has a golden horn in the middle of his forehead,' he told her. Then he went back to the garden to watch the unicorn; but the unicorn had gone away. The man sat down among the roses and went to sleep.

As soon as the husband had gone out of the house, the wife got up and dressed as fast as she could. She was very excited and there was a gloat in her eye. She telephoned the police and she telephoned a psychiatrist; she told them to hurry to her house and bring a strait-jacket. When the police and the psychiatrist arrived they sat down in chairs and looked at her, with great interest. 'My husband,' she said, 'saw a unicorn this morning.' The police looked at the psychiatrist and the psychiatrist looked at the police. 'He told me it ate a lily,' she said. The psychiatrist looked at the police and the police looked at the psychiatrist. 'He told me it had a golden horn in the middle of its forehead,' she said. At a solemn signal from the psychiatrist, the police leaped from their chairs and seized the wife. They had a hard time subduing her, for she put up a terrific struggle, but they finally subdued her. Just as they got her into the strait-jacket, the husband came back into the house.

'Did you tell your wife you saw a unicorn?' asked the police. 'Of course not,' said the husband. 'The unicorn is a mythical beast.' 'That's all I wanted to know,' said the psychiatrist. 'Take her away. I'm sorry, sir, but your wife is as crazy as a jay bird.' So they took her away, cursing and screaming, and shut her up in an institution. The husband lived happily ever after.

Moral: Don't count your boobies until they are hatched.

aus: James Thurber, The Thurber Carnival, Middlesex: Penguin repr. 1977, pp. 304f.

Quellenverzeichnis

Crowther, Jonathan (ed.), Oxford Advanced Learner's Dictionary of Current English, 5th ed., Oxford: Oxford University Press 1995

Janssen, Sigrid / Hamm, Udo, Thematischer Wortschatz Englisch, Berlin: Cornelsen & OUP 1994

Hill, L.A., Elementary Steps to Understanding, Oxford: OUP 1980

Sinclair, John / Fox, Gwyneth u.a. (eds.), Collins Cobuild Dictionary of Idioms, London: Harper Collins 1995

Stephan, Horst, Denk- und Konzentrationsaufgaben, Stuttgart / Dresden 1996

Stephan, Horst, Vertretungsstunden in der Sekundarstufe 1, Stuttgart / Dresden 1996

Terrell, Peter / Schnorr, Veronika u.a., Collins German - English / English - German Dictionary, 3rd ed., Stuttgart: Klett 1997

Thurber, James, "The Unicorn in the Garden", in ders., The Thurber Carnival, Middlesex, England: Penguin Books, repr. 1977, pp. 304f.